THE PLAY'S THE THING

A Photographic Odyssey through Theatre in San Diego

THE PLAY'S THE THING

A PHOTOGRAPHIC ODYSSEY THROUGH THEATRE IN SAN DIEGO

PHOTOGRAPHY BY
KEN JACQUES

EDITED BY DEA HURSTON
FOREWORD BY PAT LAUNER • INTRODUCTION BY SAM WOODHOUSE

SUNBELT PUBLICATIONS

San Diego, California

Sunbelt Publications, Inc.
All rights reserved. First edition 2005
Edited by Dea Hurston
Book and cover design by Laurel Miller
Production Coordinator Jennifer Redmond
Printed in the United States of America

Sunbelt Publications, Inc.
P.O. Box 191126
San Diego, CA 92159-1126
(619) 258-4911, fax: (619) 258-4916
www.sunbeltbooks.com

08 07 06 05 04   5 4 3 2 1

Library of Congress Cataloging-in-Publication Data

Jacques, Ken.
The play's the thing : a photographic odyssey through theatre in San Diego / Ken Jacques.—1st ed.
  p. cm.
1. Stage photography—California—San Diego. 2. Theater—California—San Diego—Pictorial works. 3. Jacques, Ken. I.
Title.

TR817.J33 2004
792'.09794'985022—dc22

                                                2004023233

All photographs by Ken Jacques.
Cover Photograph: Shannon Partrick in *The Secret Garden*. San Diego Junior Theatre, 2003.

This book made possible by a generous contribution to the San Diego Performing Arts League by Audrey Geisel and the Dr. Seuss Foundation.

We salute Mrs. Geisel for her many years of dedicated commitment to promote arts and culture in the greater San Diego community.

San Diego Performing Arts League

For more than twenty years, the San Diego Performing Arts

League has spread the message to residents and visitors alike that "when the sun goes down, the curtain goes up!" Through programs such as ARTS TIX, San Diego's half-price ticket booth, the *What's Playing Guide* and **www.sandiegoperforms.com**, the League has worked to promote theatre, music, and dance throughout San Diego County, while also making it accessible, affordable and appealing.

It all started in 1981, when a group of devoted theatre lovers, led by Bill Purves, met to establish a Festival of the Performing Arts. It became clear that, in order to have a festival, there had to be an organization to *produce* the festival. It turned out that more people were interested in the *organization* that would produce the festival than the festival itself.

In December of 1983, the San Diego Theatre League was born and boasted 28 member organizations. In 1986, Alan Ziter was hired as the San Diego Theatre League's first executive director and San Diego's half-price ticket booth (similar to New York City's TKTS booth) opened at its temporary location in the lobby of the Spreckels Theatre. A permanent booth was soon erected and ARTS TIX still shines brightly in the center of downtown as a beacon for the performing arts at Horton Plaza Park. In 1998, the Theatre League was renamed the San Diego Performing Arts League to better reflect the diversity of its growing membership.

The success of ARTS TIX continues to make the performing arts accessible and affordable for San Diegans and our visitors. The colorful kiosk outside of Horton Plaza and now ARTS TIX online are just some of the ways the League builds audiences and strengthens the arts. Additional programs developed over the years helped build the organization and the performing arts community, including the Arts and Business and STAR Awards, a celebration of volunteers in the performing arts.

Growth and change continue for the San Diego Performing Arts League. The organization and its growing membership of music, dance, and theatre groups is ready to move forward to "promote and advance the performing arts" for the next 20 years.

We'll see you at the theatre!

Stephanie Casenza
Executive Director

Sales of this book benefit the San Diego Performing Arts League, a non-profit arts organization whose mission is to promote and advance the performing arts.

Foreword

There were still cows grazing in Mission Valley in 1975. By the time I moved to San Diego from New York in 1979, the cows were out, the Mall was in, and the county population was over a million strong (it's now almost 4 million). But San Diego still had a small-town mentality—which was good and bad. It was thought of as a Navy town, a bastion of conservatism, a beach community. The burgeoning arts scene was still blotted out by the sun.

But for theater-lovers, the '80s was a thrilling era of growth and experimentation. The Old Globe had three theaters in place, with Jack O'Brien joining Craig Noel at the helm. The La Jolla Playhouse was revitalized when Des McAnuff strode into town and changed the La Jolla landscape. And smaller companies were blossoming, too. Lamb's Players Theatre started its robust resident ensemble. The Gaslamp Quarter Theatre Company and the San Diego Repertory Theatre were making waves. Outdoor venues were attracting crowds to watch musicals by Moonlight or Starlight. The Bowery Theatre (which became Blackfriars) was drawing non-mainstream audiences to its quirky productions in funky spaces and, later, the Fritz Theater did the same. And Sledgehammer pummeled its way into people's hearts. By 1987, the Wall Street Journal called San Diego "a theater boom-town." We started sending productions to Broadway. Two local companies (the Globe and La Jolla Playhouse) won special Tony Awards for Outstanding Regional Theater. We began to be more than just a dot on the American theater map.

I loved the big theaters, of course, but I really adored the intimate spaces and small storefront companies. I even started one of my own—Sign of the Times, the San Diego Theatre of the Deaf, which debuted in 1980, at the (now defunct) 2nd Avenue Theatre. Over time, a range of niche theaters sprang up: Teatro Máscara Mágica, Asian American Repertory Theatre, San Diego Black Ensemble Theatre, Diversionary Theatre, Women's Repertory Theatre. We were starting to act and feel like a Big City. In 1994, The New York Times said our "air is as redolent of theater as it is of the sea." In 2001, Travelocity.com called San Diego "the newest cultural Mecca in the United States."

Small companies ebbed and flowed with the economic tide and with the availability of space; as exciting as site-specific theater could be, it was hard to attract an audience without a stable home base. But theater-folk are relentlessly resilient and endlessly optimistic. They simply have to do what they love to do, and they'll do it by any means possible. They do it for love, certainly not for money. They put their hearts, guts, and ingenuity into every production, and they play devotedly even to an audience of only a handful of hearty souls. Once you develop a theatergoing habit, you're as hooked as they are.

Some people just don't realize how different theater is from movies or TV or video games. These are live people, acting right there in front of you, as you sit in a darkened room sharing the experience with other wide-eyed witnesses. Occasionally, there are onstage mistakes or technical mishaps. It's all there for you to see. No one tells you where to look or focus your attention; you can watch the lead actor, or the drooping sock on a cute chorine. You can concentrate on the set, the lighting, the background music. It's all happening in real time, before your eyes. And, as any actor will tell you, no matter how much a play is 'set' in rehearsal, no two performances are exactly the same. Because the audience responds to the actors and the players react in turn. It's a genuine interactive game, of the most rewarding kind. And it's often not just about entertainment.

Since the time of the Greeks, theater has served to educate, enlighten, present other worlds and viewpoints… or, as Hamlet put it, "to hold… the mirror up to nature." It can inspire you to act, or to reconsider your place in the universe, or your relations to your mate or family. It can make you cackle or weep, but most important, at its best, theater forces you to think. Stimulating plays have raised issues, questions, and concerns that have kept me lingering in the lobby long after a show, and the conversation often continues, with my husband, well into the night.

Years ago, I began to measure my life in plays. Particular productions—hilarious, tear-jerking, gut-wrenching or otherwise unforgettable—have become my milestones and markers. They trigger mental images, memories, and emotions.

But theater is an ephemeral artform—a whisper on the wind, a flash of brilliance that vanishes as soon as the curtain falls…

So I was ecstatic to learn that Ken Jacques, who started marking his life in productions just about the same time I did, had decided to publish the heart-stopping moments of San Diego theater that he'd captured and recorded over the years. Ken doesn't just go to shoot those shows as a hired gun; he loves the theater as much as any of us, and celebrates the genius that goes into making the magic. His photographs offer a glimpse of history, energy, talent, passion and creativity. They pierce the heart and touch the soul. Looking at each page, each gorgeous, evocative image, stops my breath and recreates the emotion of the experience. This book is a feast for all the senses. So feed your habit and feed your head… and if I don't see you at the theater, I'm sure to run into you on Memory Lane.

Pat Launer
Theatre Critic
October, 2004

Introduction

Wonderfully visceral photographs send me immediately back into the sense memory of a distinctive theatrical production. My ears recall the slap or elegance of the play's language. My eyes recapture a terrifying or gorgeous image. My skin trembles with the resurrection of a chill or a gush provoked by an electric moment in the theatre. If the production was that rare miracle that is today "unforgettable" in my memory, a vibrant and inspired photograph can provoke even *my* heart to open and blush and remember.

Great theatrical photographs can capture the burning desire that every great actor brings to the quest of a character. Great theatre photographs can capture the thrill of the great actor's reach into the unknown that is central to every great performance. Great theatre photos can memorialize the moments of unscripted intimacy that every great actor lives for. Great theatre photographs are as rare as great plays, great productions, and great loves.

Thanks to Ken Jacques, each of us has the good fortune to recall and assemble our own unforgettable list of great San Diego theatre memories. We are blessed to have the luxury of choosing from 22 years of Ken Jacques photographs our own very personal collection of great theatrical moments of wonder.

Thank you, Ken. Because of you our sense memories are nurtured.

Sam Woodhouse
Artistic Director
San Diego Repertory Theatre

Preface

As I sit here choosing a couple hundred photographs from over 1,200 for this book, I am being taken on an incredible journey—getting the chance to revisit some fantastic pieces of work that have occurred on the many stages here in San Diego. I am also reminded of how I got the chance to be a part of this industry, too, as a different kind of Storyteller.

It was 1982. I was this ex-archaeologist, a struggling new photographer trying to get established. But I had yet to find the area of photography that really interested me. Not family portraits, not Grip & Grins. I was looking for a realm that would fuel my passions, and produce that intangible feeling that fires the excitement of work. Months went by and I was losing hope of finding *it*, wondering if I'd made a mistake and wasted everyone's time and mine...Then the phone call came that changed everything.

My friend, an English teacher from Hilltop Junior High School, was in a new play at The Bowery Theatre in downtown San Diego. She knew I was a photographer, but didn't know that my confidence had hit an all-time low. She needed someone to shoot the publicity photos for the production. I did not have a clue as to what that meant, but I wanted in—and I went in with everything I had.

The shoot went better than I could have ever imagined, and I have a very good imagination. For days afterward I was up in the clouds, my feet never touching the ground. *I had found it*! I knew that this was what I wanted to do.

Jeff Smith at the *Reader* called me up ask why I was not shooting for other theatres. I explained that this was my first attempt at it, but I wanted more. He said that he would call the Old Globe, The Rep, and Starlight. Soon I had a call from Craig Noel, asking me to shoot *Rashomon* (their 200th production), and as they say, the rest is history. Thank you Jeff!

A good portion of the images in this book are black and white. One reason is that we photographed many of the early productions in b&w out of economic necessity. Another reason was that back then the local newspapers were not printing in color. (Some theatres wanted color and b&w—so I shot both.) But for me there was another, more visceral, reason why I enjoyed working in b&w; growing up I had a fascination with the great photographers from the Hollywood glamour days, with their rich b&w images. Wonderful textures and layers of contrast combined with skillful lighting—something that I had found again in the theatre.

Now, with the growth of digital imagery, I'm like a kid in the candy store. There are so many wonderful ways to use this technology and I am very excited about exploring new opportunities with the tradition of the theatre and this new technology.

It's my sincere hope as you prepare to view this book that you have a sense of anticipation—just like when you sit in your seat waiting for the start of a play...That you are taken on a journey. And that the journey engenders fond memories of some of the great Storytellers of the live stage here in our own San Diego.

Acknowledgements

With a project this size there are so many people that I want to thank. As I look back at this part of my career I realize that I could not have done any of this without my God guiding me. Sharon, who has been with me for this journey, helping me, sharing the ride, always believing in me, and always patient with my crazy schedule—thank you. Jeff Smith, who made that first call to say, "you need to do more of this." Dea Hurston, who embraced this book as if it were her own. Jennifer Redmond, who wanted this book almost as much as I did. Mom, who toiled in the dark room all of those years. For my friends Teresa and Dave, who always said that if I want it then I should just do it. Ed Hoffmiester, for always being there to help. Brian Salmon, who was not only a contributor, but was in on the great search for lost names. Deb and Bob Smyth for your kindness and belief in me. Nate Pierson, for shooting the photo of me for the book cover. Pat Launer and Sam Woodhouse—thank you!

A special thank you goes to the amazing community of talented artists who contributed their memories to this book; to the many theatres that have embraced my work; to all of the artists who put their heart and talents on the stages of San Diego every night to bring the stories to life; to the directors, designers, playwrights, and especially the patrons.

A few of the Storytellers have passed away from our stages. Although they are no longer with us I still have wonderful memories of the work they did to bring these theatres to life. Thank you: Kent Bennidict, Will Roberson, Ron Taylor, Damon Bryant, James Hansen, and Kathryn Faulkner. You are missed.

Ken Jacques
San Diego, California
October, 2004

PLAYERS · PLAYS · PLAYHOUSES

PLAYERS

Adam Lambert 30
Albert Farrar 57
Alexandra Auckland 27
Alma Martinez 132
Amanda White 41
Amy Herzberg 73
Andrea Renee 52
Andrew Fullerton 28
Andrew J. Traister 21
Andrew Nichols 60
Angie Phillips 110
Anne Gee Byrd 61
Anne Tran 40
Annie Berthiaume 135
Annie Hinton 130
Anthony De Longis 21
Antonio "TJ" Johnson 114
Arielle Turner 51
Ava Liss 78
Awet Andemicael 39
Ayla Yarkut 1
Barbara Tarbuck 90
Bekki Vallin 55
Ben Gammage 43
Bernard Baldan 11, 128
Bets Malone 82, 137
Beverly Ward 7, 82, 131
Bill Anton 23, 116
Bill Virchis 113
Bonni Ward 79
Brendan Ford 5
Brian Salmon 25, 54, 55, 60
Brian Wells 64
Camilia Sanes 70, 71
Canice Nicole 64
Cathy Gene Greenwood 38
Chad Frisque 78
Charlene Baldridge 124
Charlie Riendeau 47
Charyn Cannon 119

Cheryl Francis Harrington
   66, 67
Christopher Williams 120
Craig Noel 18, 20, 44, 59, 61,
   62, 66
Cynthia Gerber 32
Cynthia Hammond 41
D.W. Jacobs 22, 23, 85, 128
Dana Hooley 40
Dana Pere 57
Danica McKellar 6
Darla Cash 73, 74, 85
David Brannen 26, 27
David Cochran Heath 33, 50,
   122
David Ellenstein 47
David Engel 82
David Hunt 110
David Kornbluth 25
David McBean 31, 125
David McClendon 61
David S. Humphrey 114
David Tierney 144
Davis Kornbluth 25
Dawn Veree 38
Debbie Smyth 107
Deborah Gilmour Smyth 32,
   107
Deborah Van Valkenburgh 13,
   46, 58, 68
Delia MacDougall 108
Des McAnuff 71, 110
Diana Castle 73
Dianna Ruggiero 14
Dianna Sandler 78
Diep Huynh 143
Dominic Hoffman 75
Donald McClure 125
Don and Bonni Ward 79
Don R. McManus 61
Don Ward 79, 83, 88

Doren Elias 33, 114
Douglas Roberts 13, 60, 90,
   93
Douglin Murray Schmidt 78,
   89
Edward Staudenmayer 135
Erica Beth Phillips 115
Eric Anderson 3, 48, 88
Evelyn de la Rosa 39
Farhang Pernoon 104
Fernando Flores Vega 65
Floyd Gaffney 35, 74
Genna Ambatielos 58
George Gonzales 15
Gina Feliccia 48
Gordon McLachlan 45
Goyo Flores 25
Greg Thompson 33
Gustavo Halley 14
Herbert Siguenza 97
Ian Gilligan 95
J. Kenneth Campbell 20
J. Michael Ross 33
J. Sherwood Montgomery 14,
   89
Jack O'Brien 57, 58, 59, 61,
   74
Jack Tygett 44
James Callahan 61
James Cooper 64
James Hansen 24, 55
James Saba 130
James Vasquez 125
Janet Hayatshahi 144
Jason Connors 40
Jason Martin 24
Jeanne Reith 104
Jean Crupper 60
Jefferson Mays 18, 52, 53
Jeffrey Jones 130

Jeff Meek 46
Jeff Smith 18
Jennifer Austin 31, 122
Jennifer Parsons 109
Jennifer Shelton 79
Jenni Prisk 143
Jeremiah Lorenz 142
Jessa Watson 130
Jill Lewis 100
Jim Chovick 130
Jim Mooney 114
Jim Phipps 66, 67
John-Paul Baumer 28
John Bisom 30, 38
John Garcia 47
John Guth 16
John Huntington 82
John Mueller 65
John Vaughn 88
Jonathan Edzant 42
Jonathan McMurtry 5, 47, 98
Jon Lorenz 33, 50, 51
Jon Matthews 46
Jon Tenney 56
Jorge Galvan 113
Josefina Lopez 80
Joshua Carr 76
Joshua Fischel 38
Jo deWinter 37
Juan Manzo 15
Juan Monsalvez 105
Julia Giolzetti 44
Julie Jacobs 69
Justin Robertson 30, 48
Jyl Kaneshiro 47
Karen Ann Daniels 95
Karl Backus 104
Karole Foreman 28, 77, 119
Kathi Gibbs 34
Katherine McGrath 98

Kathy Brombacher 79, 83
Kathy Ireland 99
KB Mercer 28
Keith Jefferson 107
Kellie Waymire 116
Kelly Ward 131
Kent Benedict 17
Ken Jacques xi
Kerry Mead 51
Kevin Spirtas 49
Kim McCallum 25, 54, 55, 60
Kirby Ward 7, 43, 131
Kirsten Benton Chandler 140,
   141
Kirsten Brant 92
Lakin Valdez 132
Lance Roberts 79
Lance Rogers 28
Laura Bozanich 143
Laurel Johnson 54
Lauren Hasson 17
Laurie Lehmann-Gray 40
Lawrence E. Johnson, Jr. 52
Lawrence Hecht 109
Leigh Scarritt 76, 137
Leon Natker 39
Linda Castro 40
Linda Hoy 57
Linda Libby 11, 96, 114, 136
Linda Williams Janke 99
Lisa Drummond 50, 51
Lisa H. Payton 119
Liv Kellgren 40
Lizbeth Mackay 10
Lois Markle 99
Lucy Rodriguez 80
Luis Antonio Ramos 70, 71
Lupe Ontiveros 80
Lynn Wood 37
Mark Christopher Lawrence 84

PLAYERS

Marty Hrejsa 47
Matte Osian 91
Matthew Bohrer 42
Matt Scott 122
Megan Weston 14, 78
Melinda Gilb 2, 58, 59
Michael Baumann 73
Michele Mais 72
Michi Barall 52
Mikael Salazar 68
Mike Buckley 50
Mike Genovese 90
Misty Cotton 30
Mitchell Edmonds 20
Monica Quintanilla 119
Monica Schneider 9
Monique Fowler 56
Natalie Turman 41
Nick Cordileone 1, 32, 84
Norman Large 2
Ole Kittleson 64

Ollie Nash 18, 111
Osayandi Baruti 72
Pace Ebbeson 108
Pamela Turner Heath 51
Pam Kragen 110
Patrick Dollaghan 74
Pat DiMeo 28
Pat Launer 86, viii
Paul Eggington 106
Paul James Kruse 65
Paul Maley 95
Peggy Blow 119
Peter Jacobs 36
Priscilla Allen 12, 13, 26, 82, 143
Ralitza 36
Ralph Elias 120
Rebecca Stanley 37
Ria Carey 100
Richard Farrell 73
Richard Israel 137

Richard Kneeland 66, 67, 124
Richard Montoya 97
Rick D. Meads 84, 122
Ric Salinas 97
Roberta Maxwell 21
Robert Foxworth 134
Robert Grossman 120
Robert Smyth 32, 106, 107, 122
Robert Townsend 58, 137
Robin Gammell 134
Ron Campbell 68, 69, 111
Ron Taylor 129, x
Rose Weaver 67
Rosina Reynolds 5, 63
Roxane Carrasco 80
Ryan Drummond 50, 51, 84
Ryan Wagner 44
Sabrina LaBeauf 91
Sam Woodhouse 6, 22, 36, 52, 53, 59, 72, 74, 96, x

Sandy Campbell 16, 50
Sean Murray 16, 23, 72, 77, 104, 130
Seema Sueko 136
Shana Wride 11, 59
Shannon Partrick 45, cover
Spencer Moses 31
Stan Chandler 102
Stephanie Ward 45
Stephen Godwin 115
Stephen Reynolds 8
Steven Bray 125
Steve Glaudini 9, 48, 82, 88
Steve Gunderson 58, 59
Steve Lawrence 30
Susannah Hall 3
Susan Mosher 59
Susan Thompson 24
Sylvia M'Lafi Thompson 34, 74, 75
T.J. Johnson 115

T. Eric Hart 135
Tammy T. Casey 41
Tavis Ross 23, 73
Thomas Patrick 30
Tim Dahlberg 93
Tom Hall 67
Tom Stephenson 4, 106, 133
Tom Zohar 120
Tracey Hughes 50
Victoria Strong 102
Vic Trevino 108, 109
Walter Murray 33
Wayne Tibbits 69
Welton Jones 69, 128
Will Neblett 43
Yolanda Lloyd Delgado 105

PLAYS

1776 4, 64
Ain't Misbehavin' 141
Antigone 17
Art 106
As Bees in Honey Drown 28
Avenue X. 118
A Chorus Line 49
A Christmas Carol 59, 110, 127, 128
A Funny Thing Happened on the Way to the Forum 82, 88
A Streetcar Named Desire 91
Bent 86
Bessie's Blues 101
Boy 52
Breakfast with Les and Bess 61
Buddy…The Buddy Holly Story 65
Burn This 46
Cabaret 3, 77, 142
Carousel 88
Children of a Lesser God 36
Children of Eden 82
Cloud Tectonics 70, 71
Company 49

Cotton Patch Gospel 84
Crowns 119
Culture Clash in Bordertown 97
Damn Yankees 9
Dark as Night 112
Death of a Salesman 90
Deporting the Divas 15
Detective Story 33
Dial M for Murder 122
Die Fledermaus 39
Diversionary Theatre 62, 104
Dr. Faustus 133
Dracul 87
Eleanor 63
El Paso Blue 108, 109
Evita 76
Extremities 73
Faith Healer 10
Festival of Christmas 50, 51
Fiddler on the Roof 8
Flyin' West 74, 75
Footloose 42

For Colored Girls Who Have Considered Suicide When the Rainbow is Enuf 34
Grease 30
Gross Indecency: The Three Trials of Oscar Wilde 104
Hamlet 1, 18, 33, 52, 53
Holiday Memories 28
Holy Ghosts 18, 19
How I Learned to Drive 109
If the Shoe Fits 125
Installation 121
It Ain't Nothin' But the Blues 129
I Love You, You're Perfect, Now Change 58
Julius Caesar 134
K2 22
Key Exchange 24
Kimberly Akimbo 40
Kiss Me, Kate 102
Leonce and Lena 29
Little Shop of Horrors 73
Lone Star and Laundry and Bourbon 93
Long Day's Journey into Night 5
Lot's Daughters 62

PLAYS

Man of La Mancha 16, 48
Marriage is Forever 105
Memoir 98
Me and My Girl 26, 27
Mummified Deer 132
My One and Only 7, 83
On the Verge or The Geography of Yearning 37
Otherwise Engaged 60
Pageant 94
Picasso at the Lapin Agile 68, 69
Pinocchio 43
Private Lives 32
Proof 6
Quilters 103
R. Buckminster Fuller: The History (and Mystery) of the Universe 111
Ragtime 79
Rashomon 20, 21
Real Women Have Curves 80
Rebel Armies Deep into Chad 66, 67
Remains 136
Romeo and Juliet 44, 56, 57
Ruby's Bucket of Blood 41
Seussical 42
Singin' in the Rain 83, 131

Sisters 34
Six Women with Brain Death, or Expiring Minds Want to Know 96
Sky Girls 139
Slam 103
Smokey Joe's Café 102
South Pacific 114, 115
Suds 58, 59
Sweeney Todd 2, 38
Sweet Charity 140, 141
Sylvia 34, 74, 75, 116
Thérèse Raquin 110
The Abduction from the Seraglio 14
The Beauty Queen of Leenane 12, 13
The Beggar's Opera. 78
The Boyfriend 100
The Boys Next Door 107
The Boy Who Fell into a Book 95
The Chosen 120
The Divine Comedy. 84
The Game of Love and Chance 31
The Gondoliers 14
The Great Divorce 133
The Importance of Being Earnest 130
The Killing of Sister George 143

The Maids 40
The Pirates of Penzance 89
The Rocky Horror Show 72
The Scarlet Pimpernel 135
The Secret Garden 45, cover
The Sound of Music 45
The Strange Case of Dr. Jekyll and Mr. Hyde 111
The Time of Your Life 23
The Tooth of Crime 23
The Wager 25
The Women 81
Three Hotels 85
Three Mo' Divas 138
Three Tall Women 99
Travesties 130
Triple Espresso 83
Triumph of Love 137
Wait Until Dark 47
When You Comin' Back, Red Ryder? 54, 55
Women Who Steal 11
Zoot Suit 113

PLAYHOUSES

6th @ Penn 40
6th Avenue Playhouse 121
Diversionary Theatre 15, 62, 104, 143
FBN Productions 87
Horton Grand Theatre 83
Lamb's Players Theatre 1, 4, 32, 33, 50, 51, 84, 95, 106, 107, 114, 115, 122, 133
La Jolla Playhouse 18, 52, 62, 68, 70, 71
Lyceum Theatre 69, 87
Lyric Opera San Diego 14, 39, 78, 89, 100
Mo'olelo Performing Arts Company 136
Moonlight Stage Productions 3, 7, 30, 31, 38, 48, 79, 82, 83, 88, 102, 117, 131, 140, 141

North Coast Repertory Theatre 16, 28, 47, 63, 94, 120, 130, 142
Old Globe Theatre 10, 20, 21, 26, 37, 56, 57, 61, 62, 66, 67, 98, 113, 116, 125, 134, 139
Renaissance Theatre Company 5
San Diego Junior Theatre 42–45, 82
San Diego Repertory Theatre 6, 11, 12, 13, 18, 19, 22, 23, 36, 41, 46, 52, 53, 58, 59, 65, 68, 69, 72, 73, 74, 75, 77, 80, 81, 85, 90, 91, 96, 97, 99, 101, 103, 105, 108, 109, 110, 111, 113, 118, 119, 126, 129, 132, 138
Sledgehammer Theatre 29, 92, 112, 144
Southeast Community Theatre 34, 35
Starlight Musical Theatre 2, 8, 9, 26, 27, 49, 64, 76, 135, 137
The Bowery Theatre 17, 24, 25, 54, 55, 60, 86, 93

Ayla Yarkut and Nick Cordileone in Hamlet. *Lamb's Players Theatre, 2004.*

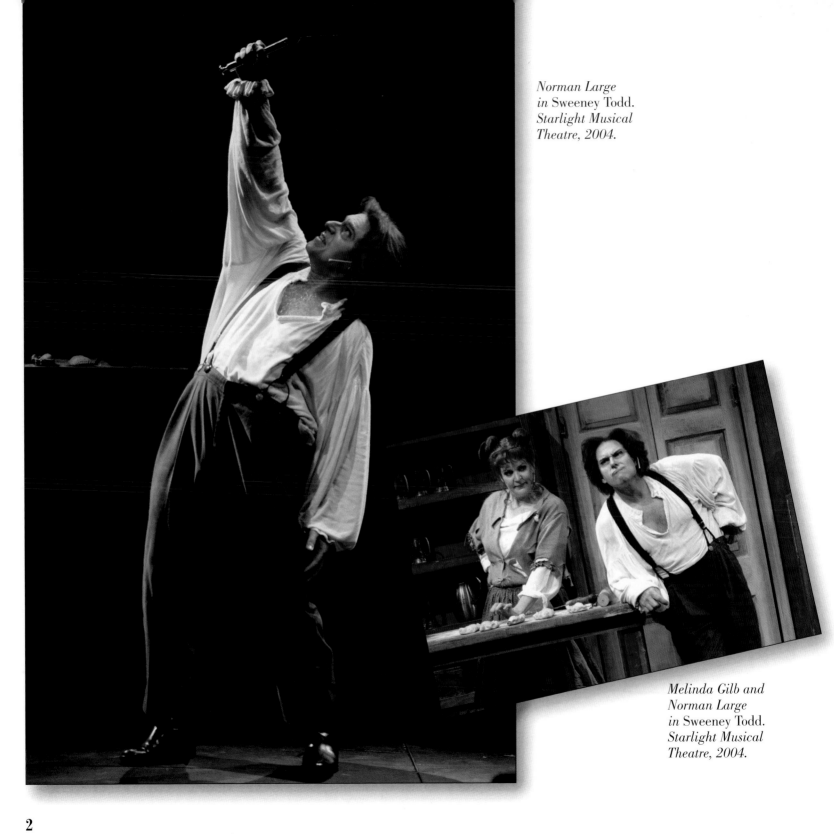

*Norman Large
in* Sweeney Todd.
*Starlight Musical
Theatre, 2004.*

*Melinda Gilb and
Norman Large
in* Sweeney Todd.
*Starlight Musical
Theatre, 2004.*

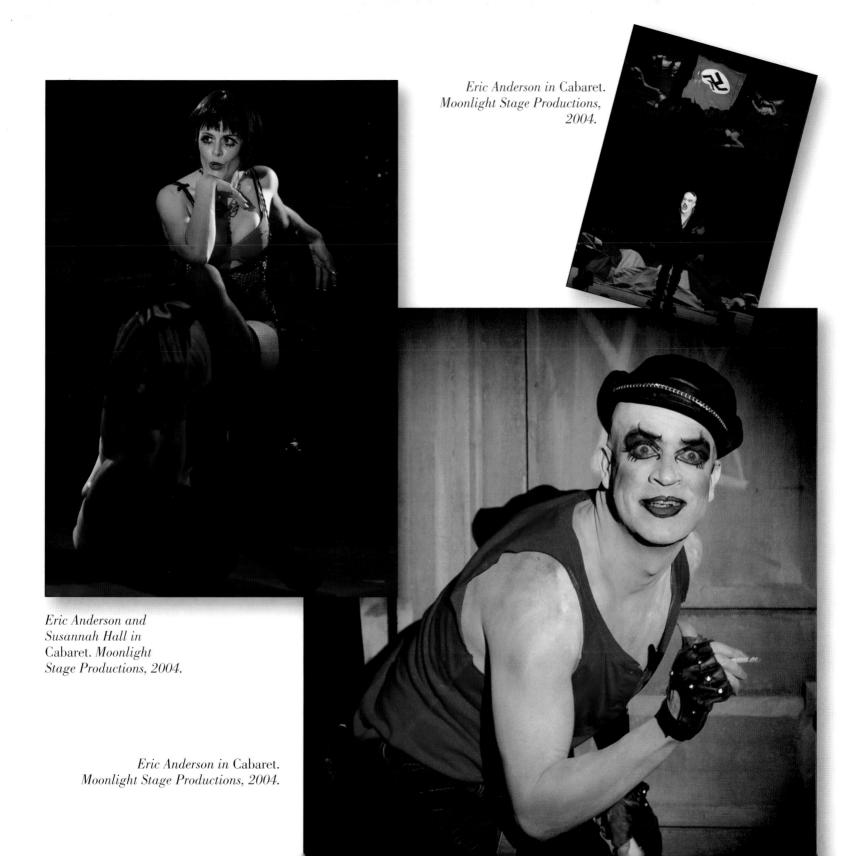

Eric Anderson in Cabaret. *Moonlight Stage Productions, 2004.*

Eric Anderson and Susannah Hall in Cabaret. *Moonlight Stage Productions, 2004.*

Eric Anderson in Cabaret. *Moonlight Stage Productions, 2004.*

Tom Stephenson in 1776.
Lamb's Players Theatre, 2003.

The Company of 1776. Lamb's Players Theatre, 2003.

4

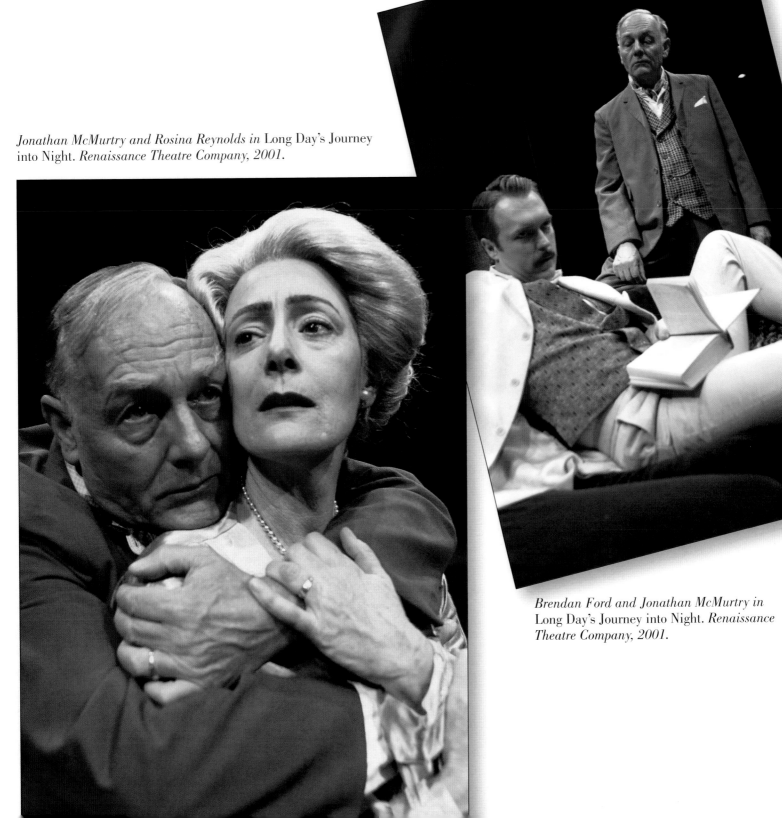

Jonathan McMurtry and Rosina Reynolds in Long Day's Journey into Night. *Renaissance Theatre Company, 2001.*

Brendan Ford and Jonathan McMurtry in Long Day's Journey into Night. *Renaissance Theatre Company, 2001.*

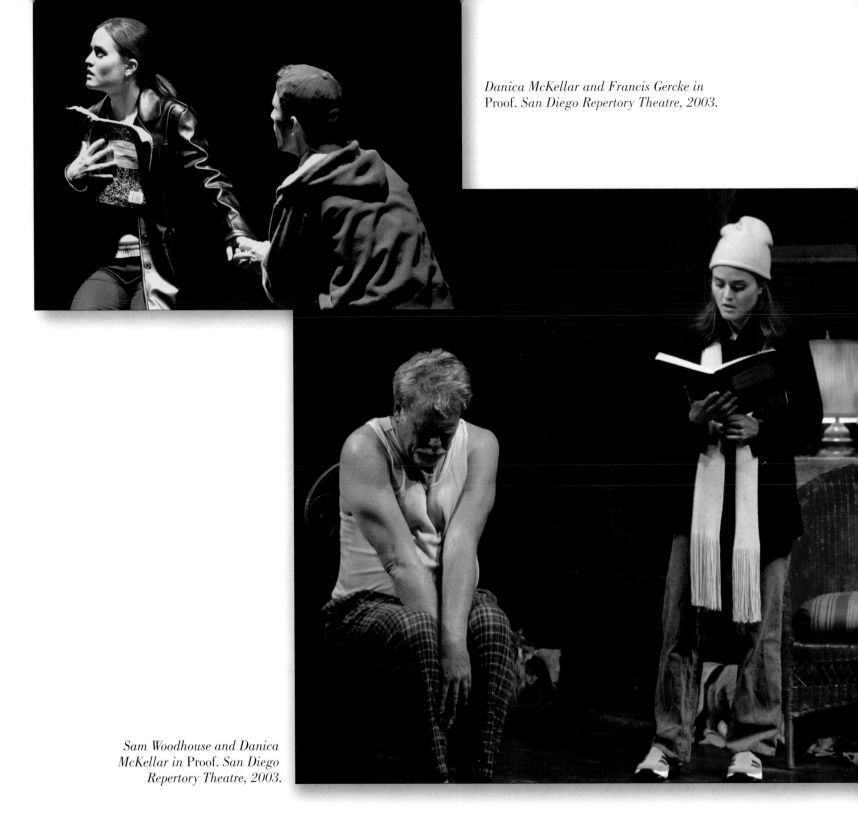

Danica McKellar and Francis Gercke in Proof. *San Diego Repertory Theatre, 2003.*

Sam Woodhouse and Danica McKellar in Proof. *San Diego Repertory Theatre, 2003.*

Above: Beverly Ward and Kirby Ward in My One and Only. *Moonlight Stage Productions, 2004.*
Below: Kirby Ward and Don Ward in My One and Only. *Moonlight Stage Productions, 2004.*

Beverly Ward in My One and Only. *Moonlight Stage Productions, 2004.*

Stephen Reynolds in Fiddler on the Roof. Starlight Musical Theatre, 2003.

Monica Schneider and Steve Glaudini in Damn Yankees. *Starlight Musical Theatre, 2004.*

9

Lizbeth Mackay in Faith Healer.
Old Globe Theatre, 2002.

10

Kinan Valdez and
Daniel Rangel in
Earthquake Sun.
San Diego Repertory
Theatre, 2004.

Linda Libby, Bernard Baldan and Shana Wride in Women Who Steal.
San Diego Repertory Theatre, 2004.

Priscilla Allen in The Beauty Queen of Leenane. *San Diego Repertory Theatre, 2001.*

Priscilla Allen, Douglas Roberts and Deborah Van Valkenburgh in The Beauty Queen of Leenane. *San Diego Repertory Theatre, 2001.*

13

*J. Sherwood Montgomery and
Dianna Ruggiero in* The Gondoliers.
Lyric Opera San Diego, 2001.

*Megan Weston and Gustavo Halley
in* The Abduction from the Seraglio.
Lyric Opera San Diego, 2003.

Juan Manzo and George Gonzales in Deporting the Divas. *Diversionary Theatre, 2003.*

Sean Murray and John Guth in
Man of La Mancha. *North Coast Repertory Theatre, 2001.*

Sandy Campbell, Sean Murray and John Guth. Man of La Mancha. *North Coast Repertory Theatre, 2001.*

16

Kent Benedict and Lauren Hasson in Antigone. *The Bowery Theatre, 1982.*

Local theatre's so fragile, so hands-on, any given day can feel like the worst of times. The struggle's ever-present, the castle always besieged. Thus it's a useful reminder, and a pleasure, to step back and see where we've come from.

When I joined the *Reader* in 1980, the Old Globe had recently turned professional year-round. There was no La Jolla Playhouse (that phoenix would rise in 1984), San Diego Rep performed in a converted chapel, Lambs Players was just starting to draw audiences to its small arena stage in National City, and UCSD was many years from being the third-ranked graduate program in America.

San Diego has since become one of the most flourishing — and respected — theatre communities in the country. We now send, on average, at least one show to Broadway per year. Growth has been slow and steady, and sudden.

The most extraordinary individual rise happened in 1991 when Jefferson Mays, a heretofore unknown graduate of UCSD's MFA program, electrified the brand-new Mandell Weiss Forum in Lee Blessing's *Fortinbras*. Mays played Osiric, and turned a cameo-character in *Hamlet* into an unforgettably harried, bedraggled being. His trying to make sense of the madness in "rotten" old Denmark made Osric the craziest of all. Mays won the 2004 Tony Award for best actor in the La Jolla Playhouse's *I Am My Own Wife*.

San Diego's always been blessed with visiting artists. John Goodman (1984) and Holly Hunter (1985) performed here long before they were John Goodman and Holly Hunter. We've seen the country's top designers and directors, including Peter Sellars, Anne Bogart, Robert Woodruff, (Bogart's *Strindberg Sonata* and Woodruff's *A Man's A Man*, being two of the most unforgettable productions I've ever seen). Along with growth there've been constant presences, turning in quality work for decades.

The most constant presence of all — whose direction of *Wonderful Tennessee* is another unforgettable one — is the Old Globe's theatrical wizard, Craig Noel. Local theatre began its steady rise the day Craig Noel decided to stay in San Diego. Not that the castle isn't still besieged. In fact snarling Philistines pound the gates as we speak.

— *Jeff Smith, Theatre Critic*

Ollie Nash and the Company of Holy Ghosts. *San Diego Repertory Theatre, 1986.*

The Company of Holy Ghosts. *San Diego Repertory Theatre, 1986.*

I acted in the first play at the Old Globe as a permanent theatre in 1937 (after the closing of the Exposition of 1935-36). I was an actor in 1937-38, but I was also a stage manager, helped with sets and props — I lived at the theatre! Then, when the Globe's director was called up by the Navy, I was chosen to be producing director — a job which I did, basically, for the next 65 years...(though my title changed).

Back then, there wasn't any other theatre here, and my purpose became to make San Diego a theatre town — and it took nearly a half-century to accomplish that. In 1969 we created the Cassius Carter, then after the fire we built the outdoor theatre, and when it burned we built the Lowell Davies Festival Theatre while rebuilding the Old Globe...As the Globe theatres grew, lots of other theatres sprung up...I'm happy that today, because we have more live theatre than any other city in California, San Diego can *really* be called a "theatre town."

— *Craig Noel, Executive Director, Old Globe Theatre*

Mitchell Edmonds and J. Kenneth Campbell in Rashomon. *Old Globe Theatre, 1983.*

*Anthony De Longis, Roberta Maxwell
and Andrew J. Traister in* Rashomon.
Old Globe Theatre, 1983.

*Roberta Maxwell and
Anthony De Longis in*
Rashomon. *Old Globe
Theatre, 1983.*

21

The Rep was in a huge financial crisis, really stretched out over an abyss. We were losing the use of the old Lyceum. The new Lyceum hadn't yet been fully funded. We were in the process of shrinking back from 400 seats to 200 seats. Cash flow was a disaster. I read the *K-2* script in a restaurant. Much of our work took place in restaurants. We didn't have offices with doors. Our whole staff of 8 or 10 people worked in the choir loft at the Sixth Avenue Playhouse, spilling now and then into the one and only dressing room. After reading *K-2*, I got so excited that I ran to find Sam. He was in the rehearsal space we rented in the Naval Training section of the El Cortez hotel. I said, "We have to do this play. It's about two guys hanging out over the side of a cliff above a huge abyss. It's about life and death. It's about the Rep. It's about us."

— *D.W. Jacobs,*
Actor, Playwright, Director

For 20 years D.W. Jacobs and I shared the pleasure and the pain of leading San Diego Rep from infancy to maturity. For me, no image more eloquently captures the trust, the struggle, the intimacy, and the angst of a long-term theatrical partnership. This photo, from our production of *K2*, captures two mountain climbers trapped on the face of the world's second tallest peak, faced with choices that truly are life-and-death.

— *Sam Woodhouse*
Actor, Director, Artistic Director,
San Diego Repertory Theatre

D.W. Jacobs and Sam Woodhouse in K2.
San Diego Repertory Theatre, 1984.

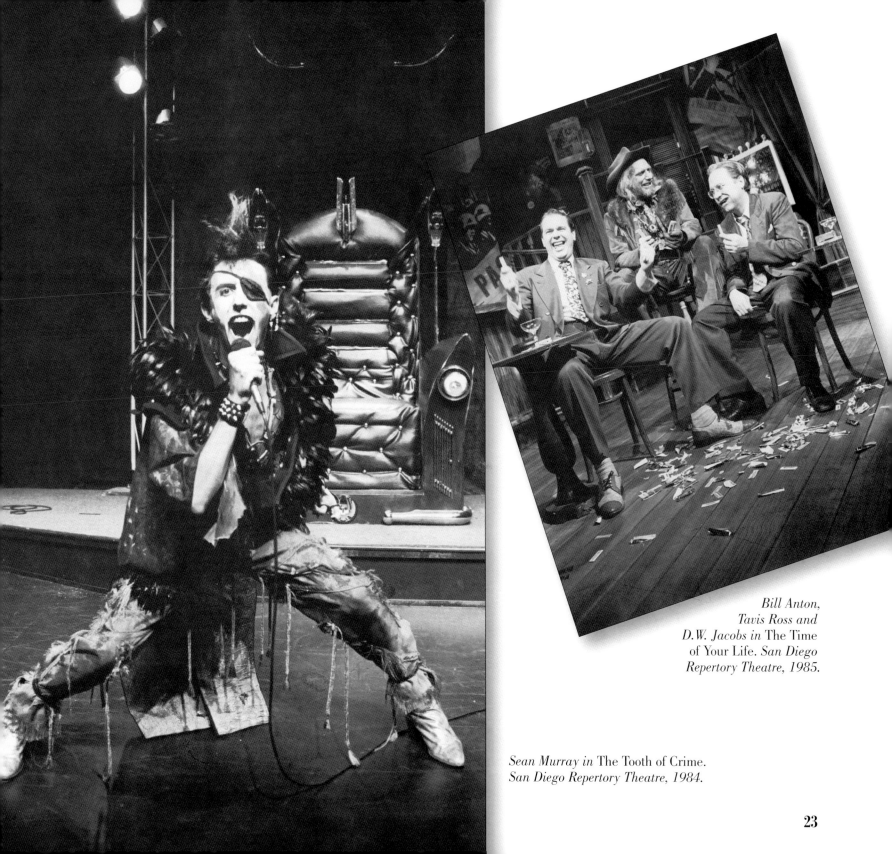

Bill Anton,
Tavis Ross and
D.W. Jacobs in The Time
of Your Life. *San Diego*
Repertory Theatre, 1985.

Sean Murray in The Tooth of Crime.
San Diego Repertory Theatre, 1984.

23

Working at the Bowery Theatre....the basement of the long term/short term, on-the-seedy- side New Palace Hotel was an exercise in....intimacy? It took extreme focus to work that close to the audience, unexpectedly improvising our way through any given performance, during the cockroach stage crossings, with the hotel residents' arguments filling (sometimes quite literally) the theatre, and for me, personally, the manueverings of that bike!...Dashing through "backstage" hotel hallways, prepping myself to ward off the personal needs of any hotel resident I might encounter, in time to make my back on stage entrance and convince the audience I had just ridden 10 miles! It was a leap of faith for all of us— certainly the audience, and it was exciting. It was, to quote my friend Jim Hansen, who shared that journey with me, "life theatre."

— *Susan Thompson, Actor*

Jason Martin, Susan Thompson and James Hansen in Key Exchange. *The Bowery Theatre, 1983.*

Right: *Susan Niweta, Kim McCallum and David Kornbluth in* The Wager. *The Bowery Theatre, 1984.*

Below: *David Kornbluth, Goyo Flores, and Kim McCallum in* The Wager. *The Bowery Theatre, 1984.*

David Brannen and Priscilla Allen in Me and My Girl. *Starlight Musical Theatre, 2001.*

I consider the Starlight Musical Theatre Company and The Old Globe Theatre the parents, if you will, of my theatre family. As a young actress attending San Diego State University, I had the good fortune of spending my summers as a cast member for these fine companies.

Happily, I still continue to work in both theatres.

When I was given the opportunity to join Actors Equity, I was told that such a membership was the "kiss of death" for an actor in San Diego. It has not proved to be so, as more and more theatres of all sizes and budgets continue to hire me as an Equity actress. I have been cast in everything, including roles written for men. Imaginative and innovative policies have kept me a busy actress for many years.

— *Priscilla Allen, Actor*

David Brannen and Alexandra Auckland in
Me and My Girl. *Starlight Musical
Theatre, 2001.*

David Brannen and Alexandra Auckland in
Me and My Girl. *Starlight Musical Theatre, 2001.*

27

Above: *KB Mercer and John-Paul Baumer in* Fuddy Meers. *North Coast Repertory Theatre, 2001.*

Below: *Karole Foreman and Andrew Fullerton in* As Bees in Honey Drown. *North Coast Repertory Theatre, 2001.*

Above: *Lance Rogers and Pat DiMeo in* Holiday Memories. *North Coast Repertory Theatre, 2001.*

Left and Below: *The Company of* Leonce and Lena. *Sledgehammer Theatre, 1990.*

John Bisom, Adam Lambert, Justin Robertson, Thomas Patrick, Steve Lawrence in Grease. *Moonlight Stage Productions, 2000.*

Misty Cotton and John Bisom in Grease. *Moonlight Stage Productions, 2000.*

30

Jennifer Austin and Spencer Moses in The Game of Love and Chance. *Moonlight Stage Productions, 2003.*

Jennifer Austin and David McBean in The Game of Love and Chance. *Moonlight Stage Productions, 2003.*

31

Deborah Gilmour Smyth and Robert Smyth in Private Lives. *Lamb's Players Theatre, 2003.*

Nick Cordileone, Cynthia Gerber and Robert Smyth in Private Lives. *Lamb's Players Theatre, 2003.*

My first experience in San Diego was after I had attended ACT in San Francisco. I came home and drifted a bit. I thought about joining the Marines, and I gave myself four months to get a job in theatre or I was off to the military. Then, as they say, fate intervened. I did a piece for the Playwrights Project in the very first year of its existence in association with the Old Globe. David Hay directed one of the plays and some time toward the end of the production, I asked him if there was any work for me at the Globe, and I meant anything. He said he would get back to me — and I ended up working three seasons at the Globe. I saw many great actors in my time there, and a couple of extraordinary ones. While I played my various spear-carrier roles, I was able to watch skilled actors like John Vickery and Brian Bedford night after night, and that was the best education a young actor could get. I cannot leave my time at the Globe without mentioning *Coriolanus*, a 1989 production I was in, which recently was named one of the best in San Diego theatre history.

After the Globe, I hooked up with Sledgehammer Theatre and man...that was a ride. Every play we did was an event; every play we produced was special and different. We moved from space to space and used the environment around us — it was great to work that way. At the time, nobody else was doing it. I also developed some great relationships with the men who founded the theatre, Scott Feldsher, Ethan Feerst, and Bruce McKenzie. We did the infamous 5-Hour *Hamlet*, a version of *Woyzec* called *Blow Out the Sun*, *Revenger's Tragedy*, and a Brecht piece, *Drums in the Night*. I believe each production, although not perfect, shook the rafters pretty good.

In 1994, Rhy's Green and I were doing an Athol Fugard play called *The Island* at the Lyceum. At the end of the play, Rhy's announced to the audience that they'd just seen the inaugural production of the San Diego Black Ensemble Theatre. My reaction was "What!" We went on to have 10 great years, and during that time we produced many Fugard plays including *Bozeman and Lena*, *Dead Swzwai Bonzie*, and *Statements Under the Immortality Act*. We also did *Twelve Angry Men* with a mixed gender and multiracial cast, and a successful version of the *Odd Couple*.

— *Walter Murray, Actor*

Above right: *Doren Elias, Jon Lorenz, Greg Thompson, Walter Murray in* Detective Story. *Lamb's Players Theatre 2003.*
Left: *J. Michael Ross, David Cochran Heath, Doren Elias in* Detective Story. *Lamb's Players Theatre, 2003.*

Left and opposite: *The Company of* For Colored Girls Who Have Considered Suicide When the Rainbow is Enuf. *Southeast Community Theatre, 1998.*

Sylvia M'Lafi Thompson and Kathi Gibbs in Sisters. *Southeast Community Theatre, 1998.*

I arrived in San Diego in the summer of 1971 as a founding member of the Theatre Arts Department at the University of California, along with Arthur Wagner and Eric Christmas, the late English character actor extraordinaire. We were single-minded in believing that diversity among UCSD faculty and students could only be achieved by recognizing differences, and that beliefs and traditions were rooted in performance practices, cultural aesthetics, and dramatic theories based in secular and sacred theatre rituals.

During this same period of time, I ventured into San Diego's world of non-profit theatre. (I experienced "culture shock," having arrived from a rich background and exposure to all art forms in such major cities as Cleveland, Pittsburgh, Atlanta, and New York.) There was only one African American community theatre to be found in this sprawling metropolis — Southeast Community Theatre (SECT). My association with SECT began when I directed Arthur Miller's classic drama, *Death of a Salesman*, with an all black cast. SECT had established a reputation for providing its audiences with what they desired and could find nowhere else in the city — theatre that embraced and celebrated black culture, ethnicity and heritage. It served the strategic function of showcasing the work of known and emerging playwrights and directors, and providing actors of color with a stage from which to experiment and create. I was associated with SECT as a director for approximately thirty years, and now serve as Artistic Director of Common Ground Theatre, formerly Southeast Community Theatre.

Floyd Gaffney, Artistic Director,
Common Ground Theatre

Ralitza and Peter Jacobs in
Children of a Lesser God.
San Diego Repertory Theatre, 1983.

Peter Jacobs and Ralitza in Children
of a Lesser God. *San Diego Repertory
Theatre, 1983.*

Peter Jacobs and I shared a profound journey as
we struggled to travel into the world of Ralitza,
a mercurial being who grew up in a Home for the
Deaf in Bulgaria, learned to speak her own form
of English from a 5 month, 5 hour a day, study of
American cartoons broadcast into her immigrant
apartment in Toronto, Canada and dropped into
San Diego determined to play the lead role in Mark
Medoff's unforgettable play.
— *Sam Woodhouse, Artistic Director,
San Diego Repertory Theatre*

Above and right: *Jo deWinter, Rebecca Stanley, Lynn Wood in* On the Verge or The Geography of Yearning. *Old Globe Theatre, 1986.*

Dawn Veree and John Bisom in Sweeney Todd. *Moonlight Stage Productions, 1994.*

Joshua Fischel and Cathy Gene Greenwood in Sweeney Todd. *Moonlight Stage Productions, 1994.*

38

Right: *Evelyn de la Rosa and Awet Andemicael in* Die Fledermaus. *Lyric Opera San Diego, 2003.*

Below: *Leon Natker and Evelyn de la Rosa in* Die Fledermaus. *Lyric Opera San Diego, 2003.*

In July of 1989, I was hired by the Board of Directors of the then–named "San Diego Gilbert and Sullivan Company" to be the new artistic director. We broadened the repertoire and changed the mission, to focus on the development of young professional talent.

Over the years, the success we have had has been the most satisfying part of my job. To watch singers like Andrew Richards and Priti Gandhi grow and mature from chorus members with small solos to leading principals in our company and now to international careers has made all the trials of the job worthwhile.

Recently, we changed our name again, to Lyric Opera San Diego. This was because after 11 years of trying to market "comic opera," we found too many people didn't understand the name. They thought we were a comedy club or a travesty opera company. We're eagerly anticipating the future in our new home at the Stephen and Mary Birch North Park Theatre.

—*Leon Natker, General Director, Lyric Opera, San Diego*

Jason Connors, Linda Castro and Liv Kellgren in Kimberly Akimbo. *6th @ Penn, 2003.*

Laurie Lehmann-Gray, Anne Tran and Dana Hooley in The Maids. *6th @ Penn, 2004.*

40

Natalie Turman and Tammy T. Casey in Ruby's Bucket of Blood. *San Diego Repertory Theatre, 1992.*

Amanda White and Cynthia Hammond in Ruby's Bucket of Blood. *San Diego Repertory Theatre, 1992.*

41

The Company of Footloose.
San Diego Junior Theatre,
2003.

Matthew Bohrer and
Jonathan Edzant in Seussical.
San Diego Junior Theatre, 2004.

San Diego Junior Theatre (JT) began its life as 'the Junior Theatre Wing of the Old Globe" in 1948. During the 1950s,'60s and '70s Junior Theatre was *the* youth theatre for San Diego. Run by the Parks and Recreation Department and competently led by Don Ward, JT had a strong reputation in the community and produced some amazing talents, among them Raquel Welch, Brian Stokes Mitchell and Kirby Ward, all Broadway headliners.

Junior Theatre's growth in the 1990s coincided with the general change in attitude toward downtown San Diego. For decades, downtown acted as the repelling pole of a magnet. No one wanted to live there and theatre artists found the area barren. By the mid '90s the polarity of the magnet had reversed, and downtown was attracting residents and a thriving local arts scene. This attraction to downtown has led to larger audiences and students for Junior Theatre, as well as a pool of quality teaching artists for classes, as well as musicians, scenic and lighting designers, and costumers for productions. The Casa del Prado Theatre in Balboa Park is still going strong and JT's satellite location, the Theatre On Third, in Chula Vista, opened in 2002, providing classes and performances in a black-box theatre setting.

— *Will Neblett, Executive Director,*
San Diego Junior Theatre

Ben Gammage in Pinocchio.
San Diego Junior Theatre, 2002.

I was visiting Craig Noel in his temporary office (due to the fire) at the Old Globe when Bill Rush passed through and urged us to go check out the outrageous performance of the kid playing the lead role in the current production at Junior Theatre. I had little time for checking out raw talent, so I didn't bother. A few days later, a young boy appeared at my rehearsal for *Godspell* asking if I had any parts open. I responded that casting was complete but if he filled out an application, I would be happy to keep him in mind for the future. When he handed back the application, I recognized the name as the kid Bill Rush had raved about. On an impulse, I let him join the cast as an understudy. The show played for two seasons at the Old Globe, during which time this lad played every male character in the show. Thus began the professional career of Brian Stokes Mitchell.

— *Jack Tygett, Director/Choreographer*

Ryan Wagner and Julia Giolzetti in Romeo and Juliet. *San Diego Junior Theatre, 2004.*

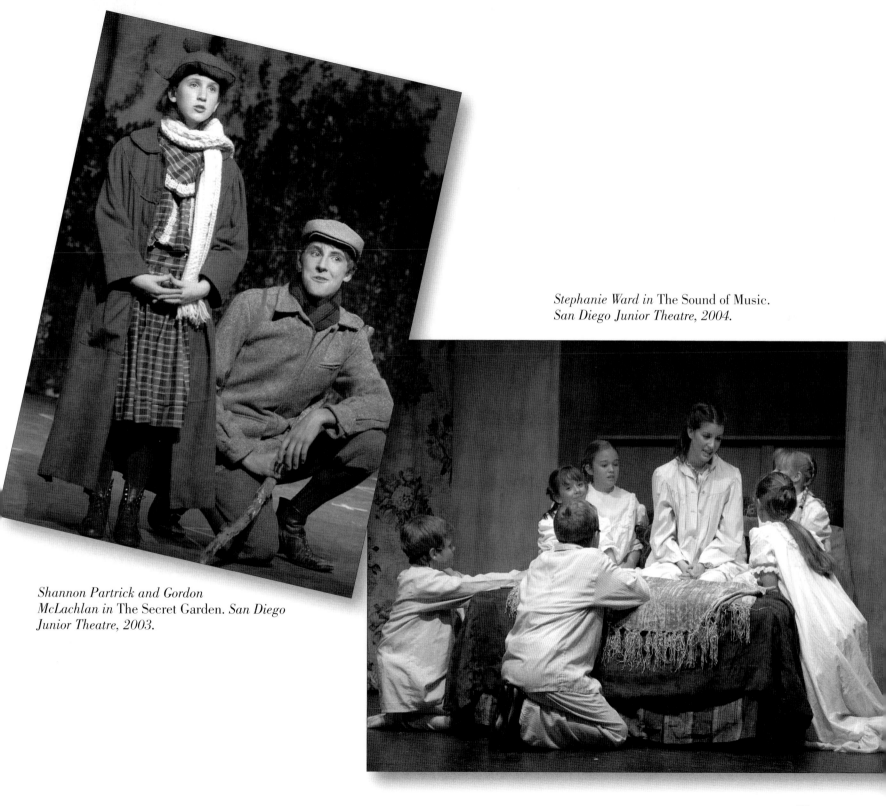

Stephanie Ward in The Sound of Music.
San Diego Junior Theatre, 2004.

*Shannon Partrick and Gordon
McLachlan in* The Secret Garden. *San Diego
Junior Theatre, 2003.*

Deborah Van Valkenburgh and Jon Matthews in Burn This. *San Diego Repertory Theatre, 1990.*

Jeff Meek and Deborah Van Valkenburgh in Burn This. *San Diego Repertory Theatre, 1990.*

46

Right: *John Garcia, Jyl Kaneshiro and Marty Hrejsa in* Wait Until Dark. *North Coast Repertory Theatre, 2000.*

Below: *Charlie Riendeau and Jyl Kaneshiro in* Wait Until Dark. *North Coast Repertory Theatre, 2000.*

My personal experience with San Diego theatre began in 1977 when I watched Jonathan McMurtry steal the show as Gremio in *The Taming of the Shrew* at the Old Globe. Though my San Diego theatre presence until recently was intermittent, I have been drawn here ever since, striving to achieve great theatre while nurturing the lives of those who are dedicated to creating it. We are lucky to live in a thriving theatre community that has only begun to fulfill its promise.

— *David Ellenstein, Artistic Director, North Coast Repertory Theatre*

47

Justin Robertson, Steve Glaudini and Eric Anderson in Man of La Mancha. *Moonlight Stage Productions, 1999.*

Above: *Eric Anderson in* Man of La Mancha. *Moonlight Stage Productions, 1999.*

Left: *Gina Feliccia, Eric Anderson and Justin Robertson in* Man of La Mancha. *Moonlight Stage Productions, 1999.*

48

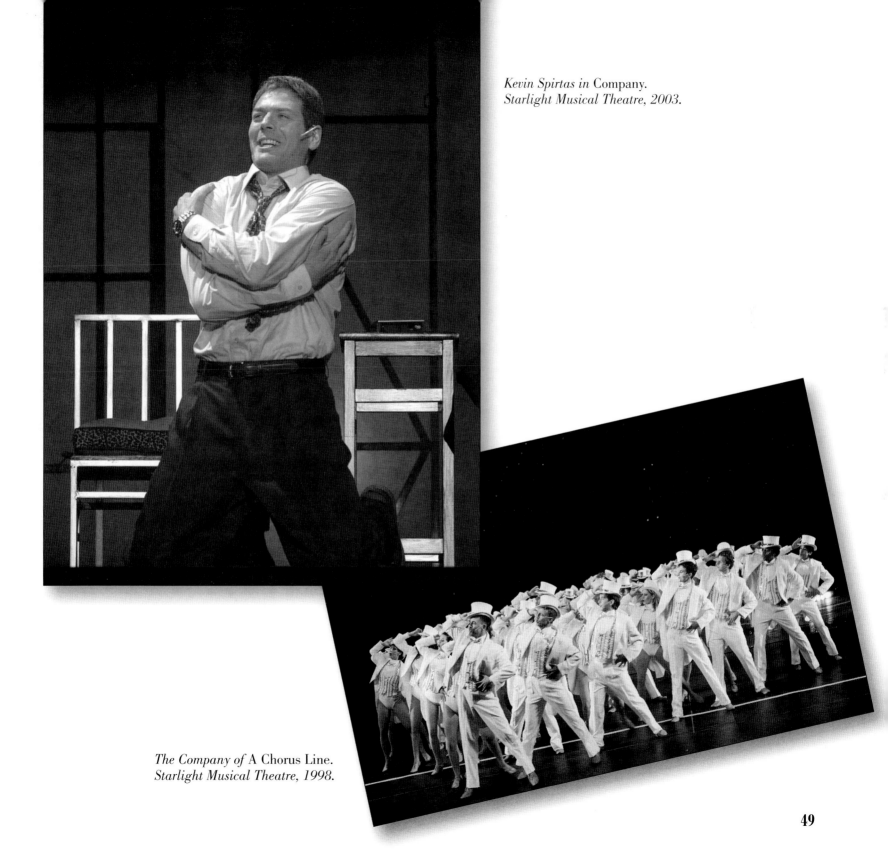

Kevin Spirtas in Company.
Starlight Musical Theatre, 2003.

The Company of A Chorus Line.
Starlight Musical Theatre, 1998.

49

The Company of Festival of Christmas. *Lamb's Players Theatre, 2000.*

Ryan Drummond, Lisa Drummond, Jon Lorenz, Sandy Campbell in Festival of Christmas. *Lamb's Players Theatre, 2003.*

Throughout these twenty years, I've been blessed to call Lamb's Players Theatre my theatrical homebase. It's a place where my penchant for wearing many different hats is not only tolerated, but encouraged, and has been a fertile pot in which to sink my roots. And it seems that Ken has always been there, clicking away at my sets, whether they're finished or not.

You see, Ken comes to take the press photos during the last dress rehearsal before previews, but my sets are often not completed until the last minutes before opening night, so I'm afraid I haven't always been delighted to see Ken show up. More than once he's been greeted with, "Oh no! *You're* here?" He seems to take it in stride now, and I've become a little more relaxed about it as well. But if you see a picture of my set in the paper and there are no drapes on the windows, now you know why. The magic isn't done yet.

— *Mike Buckley, Set Designer,*
Lamb's Players

Tracey Hughes and David Cochran Heath in Festival of Christmas. *Lamb's Players Theatre, 2002.*

I feel incredibly fortunate to have spent my artistic life in this city. San Diego Theatre has grown up since I arrived in 1976, and I've grown with it. Resident playwrights are rare. The opportunity I've had to write for an ensemble of artists for over twenty-five years is nothing short of amazing. To witness a character, who once dared to live only in my mind's eye, wrestle itself into life on stage is my ultimate creative rush.

People often ask me how I get ideas for the plays and characters I create. Okay, I admit it! I keep a little black book — a journal of "voices" that are different from my own. I interview people, fascinating people who believe they are ordinary. I have a penchant for social history — which explains in part why *Boomers* and *American Rhythm* were conceived. I also love social interactions, and frankly, real life inspires far more interesting stories than anything I could make up.

— Kerry Meads, Playwright

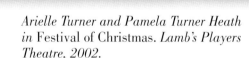

Arielle Turner and Pamela Turner Heath in Festival of Christmas. *Lamb's Players Theatre, 2002.*

Ryan Drummond, Lisa Drummond and Jon Lorenz in Festival of Christmas. *Lamb's Players Theatre, 2003.*

51

Michi Barall and Andrea Renee in Boy. *La Jolla Playhouse, 1996.*

Michi Barall in Boy. *La Jolla Playhouse, 1996.*

The Company of Boy. *La Jolla Playhouse, 1996.*

Opposite, far right: Jefferson Mays, Lawrence E. Johnson, Jr. and Sam Woodhouse in Hamlet. *San Diego Repertory Theatre, 1995. Opposite, right: Jefferson Mays in* Hamlet. *San Diego Repertory Theatre, 1995.*

One of my very favorite "scenes" is captured here in a photo from San Diego Rep's production of Hamlet, with Jefferson Mays in the title role and myself as the Gravedigger. I am forever grateful to have played up close and personal for 32 performances with one of America's greatest actors. One Sunday night, so enjoying watching Jefferson once again surprise me with his onstage choices, I forgot that the play could not go on until the Gravedigger tosses the skull of Yorick to Hamlet. The play did indeed stop that night as I, skull in hand, relished watching Jefferson perform. Hamlet began to whistle, then grin and whistle, and then grin and whistle and dance. Eventually, the Gravedigger broke from his reverie, remembered that he was indeed a character in the story and not a spectator, and tossed the skull to Hamlet. And the play did indeed, as Jefferson Mays surely has, go on.

— *Sam Woodhouse, Artistic Director,*
San Diego Repertory Theatre

I knew Kim McCallum's dad, Sandy, and Kim and I had been in a great production of *Rosenkrantz and Guildenstern are Dead*, playing the title characters. He called me up one day and said he was considering signing a lease for the basement of some hotel. He was going to turn it into a theatre space and call it "The Bowery" — essentially because that's where it was, and the name expressed his low opinion of theatres that had high opinions of themselves.

Kim quite literally built the theatre himself, carving the space out of nothing, scrounging theatre seats from the old Second Avenue Theatre and making lights from coffee cans. By the time he was through, it was really impressive. Kim and I were sitting on the bare stage one night just after he had finished. All the stage lights were on and the wooden floor he had installed was gleaming. We were talking about the shows we'd like to see happen there, and then I did the worst thing anyone can do in a theatre. I said: "Well, I think you'd make a great Macbeth." We both froze for a second and then he shoved me out the door, made me do the hokey-pokey, recite something, then knock and ask to be readmitted to the theatre. The fix seemed to work, because The Bowery really took off.

I was in both the 1983 and 1987 productions of *When You Comin' Back, Red Ryder?* They were two of the most powerful shows I've ever been involved with. The little space was packed to the rafters every night during the summer and into the Santa Anas — with no air conditioning. Audiences were moved by the show — sometimes literally. Several times, people fled across the stage during or after Kim's character Teddy's rampage in act 2. The 1983 production was so popular that I was actually cast in *A Funny Thing Happened on the Way to the Forum* at the Rep during the run of *Red Ryder*, rehearsed during the run of the show, was replaced in *Red Ryder* for the run of *Forum*, returned to *Red Ryder* and ran another six weeks.

Laurel Johnson, Kim McCallum and Brian Salmon in When You Comin' Back, Red Ryder? *The Bowery Theatre, 1983.*

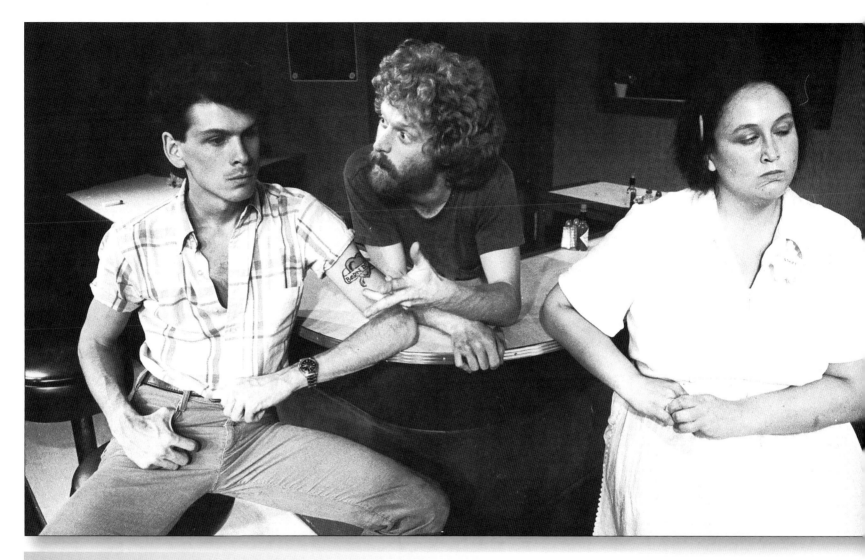

Act one of *Red Ryder* ends with my character (Richard) being shot by Kim's character (Teddy). The gun fires and the lights go out. The audience is left wondering during intermission whether the character survives. It's obviously a dramatic moment.

One night, after the regular show, we had an "actor's night" performance. Actors and crew from other shows packed the theatre. The end of act one arrived, I made a break for the door as I was supposed to, and instead of the gun firing, I heard "click." Kim tried again. "Click." And again, "click." Titters from the audience. So I turned to Kim, expecting that the stage manager would just cut the lights. Instead, Kim looked at me and yelled "BANG!" The lights went out and the audience roared.

The Bowery was a great organization with some amazingly dedicated and talented people. But above all, it was always Kim McCallum's theatre.

— *Brian Salmon, Actor*

James Hansen, Kim McCallum and Bekki Vallin in When You Comin' Back, Red Ryder? *The Bowery Theatre, 1983.*

Jon Tenney and Monique Fowler in Romeo and Juliet. *Old Globe Theatre, 1989.*

Jon Tenney and Monique Fowler in Romeo and Juliet. *Old Globe Theatre, 1989.*

56

Having San Diego as my home base has made all the difference. It's made me something of an interesting renegade... I've steadily done work in both musicals and plays and I've been able to diversify. People are amazed that I can do two projects that are quite different simultaneously, but that's what happens when you hang out at the Old Globe for twenty years.

Where else is theatre like this going to happen? It's not going to happen in New York... It won't happen in Los Angeles, because L.A. isn't live theatre, basically. San Francisco's a closed shop. We claim a territorial imperative that is ours by right, from 65 years of continuity, that rivals anyone's in the world. And our proximity to Los Angeles and the talent base is there. I have an easier time casting people in San Diego from Los Angeles than they do for theatre, because there, it represents nothing more than an audition for another film. But when they come here, they're treated seriously and they're taken seriously and they're produced beautifully. They know that.

— *Jack O'Brien,*
Artistic Director, Old Globe Theatre,
Tony-award winning director

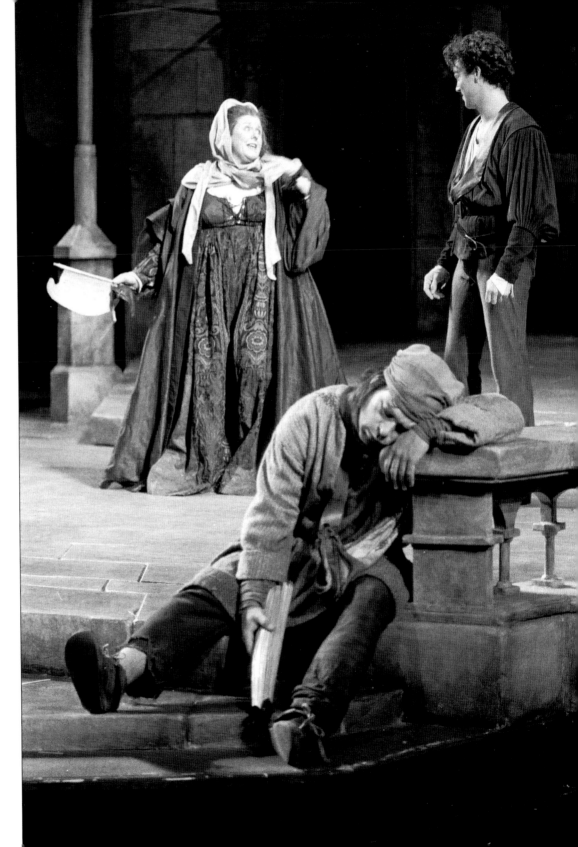

Linda Hoy, Dana Pere
and Albert Farrar in
Romeo and Juliet. *Old*
Globe Theatre, 1989.

I've had a long, wonderful history with San Diego theatre, starting with my first play at the Old Globe (*Hadrian VII*) which was — dare I say? — 30 years ago! Just a few years later my best friend Kathy Najimy and I saw a production of *A Midsummer Night's Dream* directed by Jack O'Brien that, pardon the cliché, changed our lives. It was a 'goose-bump' experience from beginning to end, and what an end! Puck delivering his last adieu and then jumping out of sight, disappearing, it seemed, into the canyon below! It took a few decades before I would finally be in a show directed by our first inspiration, Mr. O'Brien (*How the Grinch Stole Christmas*).

San Diego theatre has always been an anchor for me. Each time I work in my 'home town' it feels like a homecoming in the best way. If I had to think of one single bright spot, it would have to be *Suds*, the show I wrote with Melinda Gilb and Bryan Scott.

Genna Ambatielos and Robert Townsend in I Love You, You're Perfect, Now Change. *San Diego Repertory Theatre, 2001.*

Deborah Van Valkenburgh, Robert Townsend, Genna Ambatielos and Steve Gunderson in I Love You, You're Perfect, Now Change. *San Diego Repertory Theatre, 2001.*

58

It brought so many people into my life that continue to be friends and comrades… It brought us to the Rep and introduced me to Sam Woodhouse and Doug Jacobs, brought me back to the Globe with Craig Noel and Jack O'Brien, and it introduced me to an amazing, brilliant, fiery comet by the name of Will Roberson. He directed *Suds* and went on to direct me several more times (*The Heidi Chronicles, Only Kidding, A Christmas Carol*) as well as collaborate on a new play (*Dixie Highway*) before his untimely death. I think of him whenever a director gives me notes I don't appreciate… He used to accuse me of taking the notes that I didn't like and assimilating them in the most obvious bad actor way. He'd bark from the back of the theatre: "Steve! Just take the note!" It's become my mantra. Take the note, Steve. Thanks, Will!

—*Steve Gunderson,*
Actor, Writer, Composer

Susan Mosher, Melinda Gilb, Steve Gunderson and Shana Wride in Suds. *San Diego Repertory Theatre, 1995.*

Brian Salmon, Jean Crupper and Kim McCallum in Otherwise Engaged. *The Bowery Theatre, 1985.*

Brian Salmon, Douglas Roberts and Kim McCallum in Otherwise Engaged. *The Bowery Theatre, 1985.*

Andrew Nichols and Kim McCallum in Otherwise Engaged. *The Bowery Theatre, 1985.*

60

Anne Gee Byrd, James Callahan and Don R. McManus in Breakfast with Les and Bess. *Old Globe Theatre, 1984.*

I first became familiar with the Old Globe Theatre when I attended a talk given by Craig Noel. As a graduate directing student, I was absolutely taken by what Mr. Noel had to say, not only about the world of professional theatre, but specifically about his theatre and his town, San Diego. I liked his calm, unassuming manner and his description of his theatre and the people it attracted.

Unknown to Mr. Noel, it was at that time that I decided he was to be my mentor and it was at his theatre I would begin my career. In the remaining two years of study, I made this goal the basis for all that I did. I began a campaign of correspondence with Mr. Noel to make sure he would not forget this tenacious and probably a bit annoying young director. Mr. Noel was kind enough to allow me to come to the Old Globe to complete my studies. And what began as a six-week internship turned in to a ten-year residency as Associate Artistic Director.

With the arrival of Jack O'Brien as Artistic Director, a new, amazing era began — one that had a profound affect on us all. The scope, scale, and importance of our work increased significantly. A "Globe" style and approach to producing theatre began, which continues to have a great influence on the theatre world.

— *David McClendon,*
Artistic Director, Aspen Theatre in the Park

When I arrived in San Diego in 1978, the Old Globe had just burned down, San Diego Rep was graduating from street theatre, and the La Jolla Playhouse was yet to be reborn. With Horton Plaza just a dream, downtown San Diego looked more like East Berlin, with lonely beams of light staining the ground around the lampposts, leaving huge areas of dark and dangerous streets… but there was exciting theatre down there then.

Up in Balboa Park, Craig Noel was determined to keep the Old Globe Theatre going after the devastating fire destroyed the main stage. In those years, the Old Globe was non-union during the winter and union during the summer. I performed in my first show in San Diego on the Cassius Carter Stage — *The Misanthrope* — in the winter of 1978. Out in Spring Valley, the inimitable Frank Wayne (a refugee from New York, replete with Brooklyn accent) reigned supreme

The Company of Lot's Daughters. Diversionary Theatre, 2002.

as Artistic Director of the long-gone Fiesta Dinner Theatre and it was there that I got my Equity card in a production of *Any Wednesday*.

Downtown on 2nd Avenue was the storefront 2nd Avenue Theatre where I did my first play directed by Willie Simpson — *Uncommon Women and Others* by Wendy Wasserstein, produced by Kit Goldman for her new theatre, the Women's Theatre Ensemble. From that play began a long and enduring relationship with Willie and Kit and designer Bobby Earl, culminating in the glorious years of the Gaslamp Quarter Theatre.

I have seen small theatre companies struggle and fall, such as The Blackfriars Theatre (which evolved out of the Bowery)… or lose their space like the Fritz did. I saw the Gaslamp Quarter Theatre become two lovely spaces before failing, unable to hold out for the long-promised redevelopment of downtown… I have seen mid-sized theatres here and all over the country close, leaving an even larger separation between the big, big theatres and the small, struggling theatres.

And yet here we are again, with a resurgence of small theatre groups putting out their shingles, Renaissance Theatre, Stone Soup Theatre, Backyard Productions, and 6th@Penn to name a few. I see The North Coast Repertory Theatre easing itself into an Equity theatre; Sledgehammer leading the avant-garde way and The Diversionary growing stronger — a result of Chuck Zito's remarkable contribution. Theatre is still healthy and alive in San Diego, ever-changing, always hopeful, never dull. It's good to have been a part of it all these years.

— *Rosina Reynolds, actor*

Rosina Reynolds as Eleanor. *North Coast Repertory Theatre, 2002.*

James Cooper in 1776. Starlight Musical Theatre, 2002.

Brian Wells, Canice Nicole and Ole Kittleson in 1776. Starlight Musical Theatre, 2002.

John Mueller in Buddy…The Buddy Holly Story. *San Diego Repertory Theatre, 1997.*

John Mueller, Fernando Flores Vega and Paul James Kruse in Buddy…The Buddy Holly Story. *San Diego Repertory Theatre, 1997.*

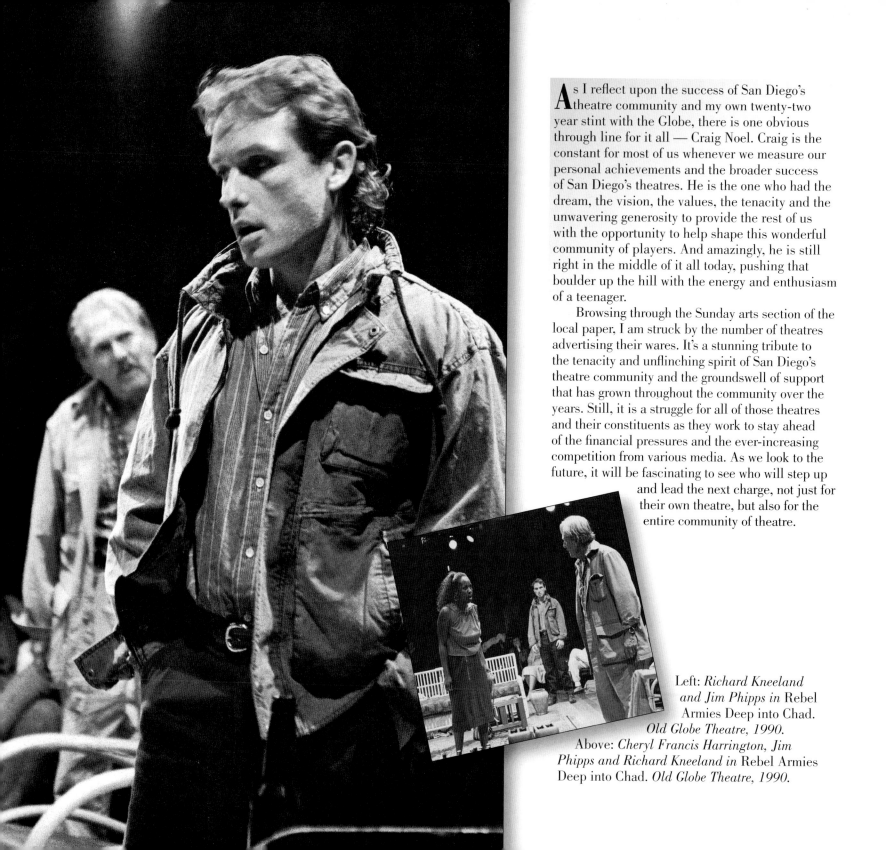

As I reflect upon the success of San Diego's theatre community and my own twenty-two year stint with the Globe, there is one obvious through line for it all — Craig Noel. Craig is the constant for most of us whenever we measure our personal achievements and the broader success of San Diego's theatres. He is the one who had the dream, the vision, the values, the tenacity and the unwavering generosity to provide the rest of us with the opportunity to help shape this wonderful community of players. And amazingly, he is still right in the middle of it all today, pushing that boulder up the hill with the energy and enthusiasm of a teenager.

Browsing through the Sunday arts section of the local paper, I am struck by the number of theatres advertising their wares. It's a stunning tribute to the tenacity and unflinching spirit of San Diego's theatre community and the groundswell of support that has grown throughout the community over the years. Still, it is a struggle for all of those theatres and their constituents as they work to stay ahead of the financial pressures and the ever-increasing competition from various media. As we look to the future, it will be fascinating to see who will step up and lead the next charge, not just for their own theatre, but also for the entire community of theatre.

Left: *Richard Kneeland and Jim Phipps in* Rebel Armies Deep into Chad. *Old Globe Theatre, 1990.*
Above: *Cheryl Francis Harrington, Jim Phipps and Richard Kneeland in* Rebel Armies Deep into Chad. *Old Globe Theatre, 1990.*

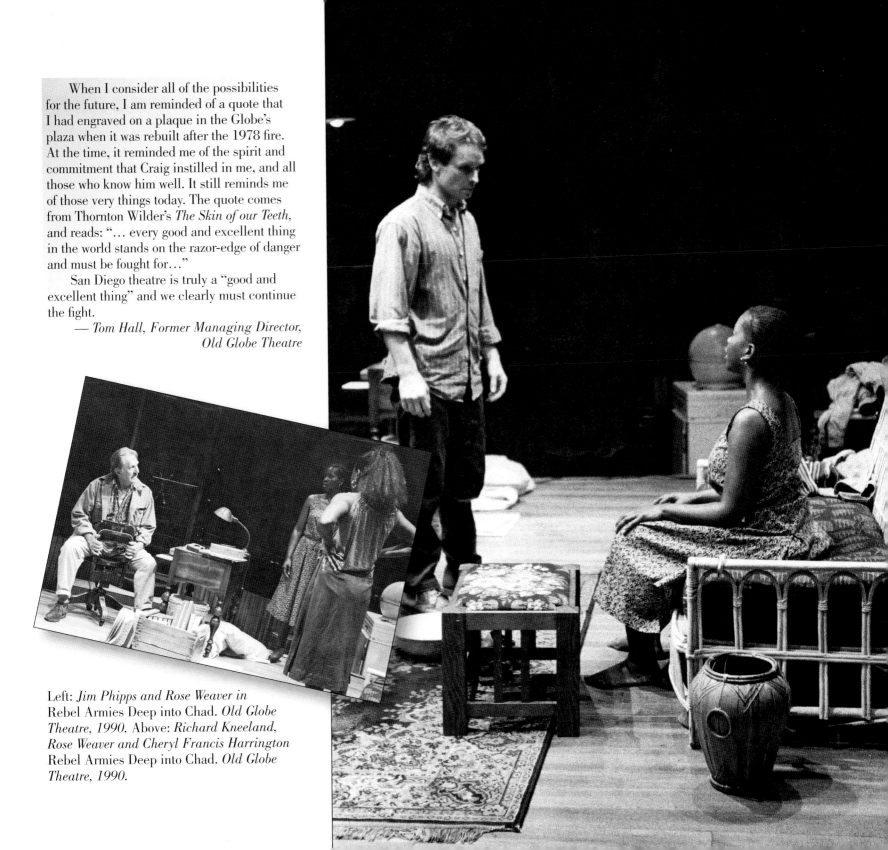

When I consider all of the possibilities for the future, I am reminded of a quote that I had engraved on a plaque in the Globe's plaza when it was rebuilt after the 1978 fire. At the time, it reminded me of the spirit and commitment that Craig instilled in me, and all those who know him well. It still reminds me of those very things today. The quote comes from Thornton Wilder's *The Skin of our Teeth*, and reads: "... every good and excellent thing in the world stands on the razor-edge of danger and must be fought for..."

San Diego theatre is truly a "good and excellent thing" and we clearly must continue the fight.

— *Tom Hall, Former Managing Director,*
Old Globe Theatre

Left: *Jim Phipps and Rose Weaver in* Rebel Armies Deep into Chad. *Old Globe Theatre, 1990.* Above: *Richard Kneeland, Rose Weaver and Cheryl Francis Harrington* Rebel Armies Deep into Chad. *Old Globe Theatre, 1990.*

Deborah Van Valkenburgh and Mikael Salazar in Picasso at the Lapin Agile. *San Diego Repertory Theatre, 1999.*

Ron Campbell and Mikael Salazar in Picasso at the Lapin Agile. *San Diego Repertory Theatre, 1999.*

San Diego was always a pretty good theatre town. In the early 20th century, the 40 thousand citizens often could choose from three resident companies and lots of touring shows.

But nothing ever happened like the last three decades, when the city's theatres grew up fast, from amateur to professional, from hobbies to tourist attractions, from recreation to art.

I remember one terribly hot summer in the 1970s, when the Globe was renovating, the Rep was still in the old funeral chapel on Sixth Avenue, the La Jolla Playhouse was a receding dream and the Fiesta Dinner Theatre was the only air conditioning on the local theatre beat. My notes from that period are still stained with perspiration.

And I remember one horrible morning about 3 when the late man on *The San Diego Union* city desk called me at home to tell me the Globe was burning. What a day! Including a city-wide power blackout while I was writing my stories. Before the sun had set, renewal was underway, Jacqueline Littlefield's offer of the Spreckels Theatre was accepted and, in three months almost to the day, the summer Shakespeare season opened in a new temporary outdoor space.

We all met to hash over such things at late-night eateries that welcomed the theatre crowd: Filippi's in Little Italy. The dear, departed Backstage Lounge adjacent to the old Lyceum Theatre. The Park Manor Hotel basement. The Jewel Box Bar. Nunu's on Fifth. Probably there's a new one now.

When I went to work reviewing shows for *The San Diego Union*, there were few theatre professionals in residence and no paid actors except in the Globe summer companies. By the time I phased out in the 1990s, there were six houses operating under contracts with Actors' Equity and a dozen more who had various agreements with Equity.

Ron Campbell, Wayne Tibbits and Julie Jacobs in Picasso at the Lapin Agile. *San Diego Repertory Theatre, 1999.*

Now there are theatres for rent, actors for hire, directors and designers building careers and audience anxious to find out what's next. Companies and individuals come and go but the audiences just continue to grow. And they support theatre companies they know will still be there the next time they're ready to see a show.

Because San Diego, even more than before, is a theatre town.

—*Welton Jones, Theatre Critic*

69

Luis Antonio Ramos and Camilia Sanes in Cloud Tectonics. *La Jolla Playhouse, 1995.*

Twenty-one years ago, as we re-opened our doors after a long hiatus, we at the new La Jolla Playhouse made a very simple choice. We decided to make it our mission to support the visions of artists and encourage them to make their own choices and fulfill their personal dreams. We focused on theatre artists without any prejudice about style or genre, recognizing that the American theatre contained a whole host of different kinds of theatre— psychological realism, magic and mythic realism, new vaudeville, post-modernism, the avant-garde and the American musical, to name just a few. It was our opinion that any truly American theatre should aspire to be able to include all of the legitimate American genres and to welcome into its ranks theatre artists who were capable of and interested in shaping the future of our artform by exploring a wide variety of theatrical pathways.

By adopting this sometimes anarchic, but almost always exciting, artistic policy, we almost instantly had an impact on the field at large. During the 1980's and 90's, several of our productions ended up on Top Ten theatre lists of national publications like *Time* magazine and the *Village Voice*. In our relatively short 21-year history, we've given world premieres to more than forty projects. Just as important, we started doing new work on a large scale along with progressive productions of classics, and what was almost unheard of for a resident theatre in the early 80's, new musicals, which we embraced as an inherent part of the American theatre repertoire.

In the 21 years since our rebirth, I think it is fair to say that La Jolla Playhouse has

played a key role in giving San Diego a national and international reputation as a vital theatre center. We have made a difference to San Diego audiences by giving them an opportunity to experience great works before they move on to New York and beyond, and having them get to know major theatre artists who now see the Playhouse as their "creative sandbox."

— *Des McAnuff, Artistic Director, La Jolla Playhouse*

Luis Antonio Ramos and Camilia Sanes in Cloud Tectonics. *La Jolla Playhouse, 1995.*

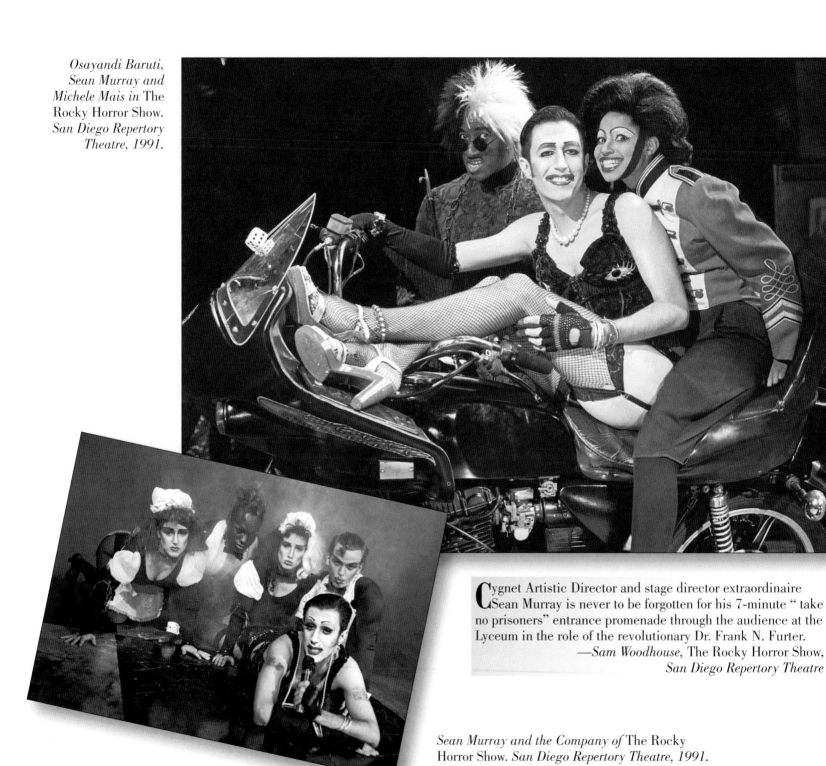

Osayandi Baruti, Sean Murray and Michele Mais in The Rocky Horror Show. *San Diego Repertory Theatre, 1991.*

Cygnet Artistic Director and stage director extraordinaire Sean Murray is never to be forgotten for his 7-minute " take no prisoners" entrance promenade through the audience at the Lyceum in the role of the revolutionary Dr. Frank N. Furter.
—*Sam Woodhouse,* The Rocky Horror Show, *San Diego Repertory Theatre*

Sean Murray and the Company of The Rocky Horror Show. *San Diego Repertory Theatre, 1991.*

Amy Herzberg, Darla Cash and Tavis Ross in Extremities. *San Diego Repertory Theatre, 1984.*

Diana Castle, Richard Farrell and Michael Baumann in Little Shop of Horrors. *San Diego Repertory Theatre, 1986.*

I can remember coming back from Paris in 1988, having followed Jack O'Brien and the cast of the Old Globe's production of *Porgy and Bess*, and getting hired as the understudy for August Wilson's *Joe Turner's Come and Gone*. I walked into the Globe for the first understudy rehearsal at 11 a.m., with my fresh new hairstyle and a smile on my face... I thought I was something, until the staff informed me I was going on *that night*. Mind you, I was going to replace Scotty Caldwell and would be onstage with Angela Basset and Delroy Lindo. That is what actors' dreams are made of, meeting the challenge. All I remember is the frenzy of the day... learning lines and blocking, the costumes and hair, someone running lines with me while I was in the bathroom...

Floyd Gaffney and Sam Woodhouse continue to make it possible for actors who do not reside in New York and Los Angeles to have respected careers, for that I am eternally grateful. Floyd Gaffney, as well as the San Diego Repertory Theatre, have risen to the challenge in San Diego, making sure that the talent that blossoms out of the African American experience is not forgotten on San Diego stages.

Flyin' West was such a special show. I have so many memories from that production. It's a rare occasion when you get to meld with the cast and become family — this was one of those times. What a joy it was to share the stage with the late Damon Bryant, my friend, my brother, my heart. It is even more rare to have such a strong role written for a woman, where the character gets to brandish a shotgun, protect her family and hear the audience shout and cheer when she stands up to the bad guy and wins! How cool is that? For this actor...very cool!

— *Sylvia M'Lafi Thompson, Actor*

Darla Cash and Patrick Dollaghan in Fool for Love. *San Diego Repertory Theatre, 1987.*

Sylvia M'Lafi Thompson and Dominic Hoffman in Flyin' West. *San Diego Repertory Theatre, 1994.*

75

The Company of Evita.
Starlight Musical Theatre, 1999.

Leigh Scarritt in Evita. Starlight
Musical Theatre, 1999.

Leigh Scarritt and Joshua Carr in Evita.
Starlight Musical Theatre, 1999.

Karole Foreman and the Company of Cabaret. *San Diego Repertory Theatre, 1996.*

Sean Murray in Cabaret. *San Diego Repertory Theatre, 1996.*

77

It was an extraordinary time in our lives in 1981 when Don and I became Starlight's artistic directors. We had been directing and choreographing for many years, our children were grown and had moved out of San Diego, and we welcomed the challenge of a 4,000 seat theatre — with airplanes!

Having loved our work with young people at Junior Theatre and touring with *The Bright Side,* we longed to provide the opportunity for those gifted young people to work side by side with established professional musical theatre performers. (Civic light operas, in our view, served as the last stepping stone to a Broadway career for young performers, much as vaudeville circuits did during the early decades of the twentieth century.)

Dianna Sandler, Chad Frisque and Megan Weston in The Beggar's Opera. *Lyric Opera San Diego, 2004.*

Ava Liss, Douglin Murray Schmidt and Dianna Sandler in The Beggar's Opera. *Lyric Opera San Diego, 2004.*

In 1994, when Starlight's Board of Directors shut down operations, Moonlight's artistic director Kathy Brombacher asked us to become involved as director and choreographer for the next season. We accepted and found that directing *Guys and Dolls* was reminiscent of Starlight during the 1950s when we were teenagers performing there. We were thrilled to be involved with Moonlight—the enthusiasm of the young people, the community pride in the operation, the support of the City of Vista and local businesses was exhilarating—and there were no airplanes! We've been an annual part of Moonlight's programming these last ten years, both at the amphitheatre and that little gem, the Avo Playhouse.

Don and I have directed at many different venues, both here and in Los Angeles, but due to our lengthy background and experience in summer musicals, outdoor venues still remain our favorite. Families can enjoy the arts together in a casual atmosphere, and share memories of warm summer nights and glorious music. We can't believe our good fortune — to have spent a good portion of our time since 1972 engaged in the joyous endeavor of mounting outdoor musical theatre productions.

> — *Don and Bonnie Ward, actor/dancers/singers,*
> *directors and choreographers*

Above: *The Company of* Ragtime. *Moonlight Stage Productions, 2002.* Right: *Lance Roberts and Jennifer Shelton in* Ragtime. *Moonlight Stage Productions, 2002.*

Lupe Ontiveros, Roxane Carrasco, Josefina Lopez, and Lucy Rodriguez in Real Women Have Curves. *San Diego Repertory Theatre, 1994.*

Lupe Ontiveros and Josefina Lopez in Real Women Have Curves. *San Diego Repertory Theatre, 1994.*

The Company of The Women. *San Diego Repertory Theatre, 1992.*

Bets Malone, John Huntington, David Engel in Children of Eden. *Moonlight Stage Productions, 2003.*

In Moonlight's first year of outdoor amphitheatre productions, Bets Malone was an 8-year-old orphan boy in our first production: *Oliver!*; and 10 years later (after many shows with Starlight, San Diego Junior Theatre, and Moonlight) she won the role of The Witch in our Southern California regional theatre debut of *Into the Woods*; in a few years she had her Equity card and has rarely had a break in her performing career. Her husband, Steve Glaudini, first performed with Moonlight in the role of Ali Hakkim in *Oklahoma!*; Bets played Ado Annie and the two of them had several hilarious scenes together. Steve did a memorable job with *The Foreigner* at our indoor Avo Playhouse; and recently starred as Pseudolus, the Slave in *A Funny Thing Happened on the Way to the Forum*, as well as Harry Houdini in *Ragtime, The Musical.* He also directed Bets in the role of Eve in the award-winning Moonlight production of *Children of Eden* in 2003.

Other memorable moments on our stage with San Diego area artists include David Brannen as Bill Snibson in *Me and My Girl*, where he played the cockney comedian to perfection, opposite the beguiling Priscilla Allen, playing his aunt, the Duchess, whose job it was to teach him the trappings of upper-class speech and heritage. The two of them brought down the house "Doin' the Lambeth Walk."

Kirby and Beverly Ward agreed to come to Moonlight four summers ago to perform together in *Crazy for You*, having starred in the national tour and the London/European productions. They came especially for the chance to work with his parents as director/choreographers, and to spend a little time in their home town of San Diego. As luck would have it, they returned in 2003 to perform on our stage in *Singin' in the Rain*, as Kathy Seldon and Don Lockwood. Their work in the dance sequences proved again that they dance as only the great dance teams of the Golden Age of Hollywood Musicals could. Our audiences were crazy for them both, along with the great team of dancers and actors behind them.

Kirby's father and mother, Don and Bonnie Ward, toured the nation as a professional dance act, and played on a bill with stars such as Mae West. Their son Kirby toured in an act with Debbie Reynolds before he married Beverly. Beverly and Kirby returned during the 2004 Summer Season to perform in *My One and Only*, where Don Ward took the role of Mr. Magix, giving the young tap-dancing aviator (Kirby) some sage advice. They brought the house down every night!

We are fortunate to have such a great heritage of superb actors who have trod the boards at Moonlight.

    —Kathy Brombacher,
        Artistic Director,
        Moonlight Stage
        Productions

Above and below left: *The Company of* Triple Espresso. *Horton Grand Theatre, 2000.*

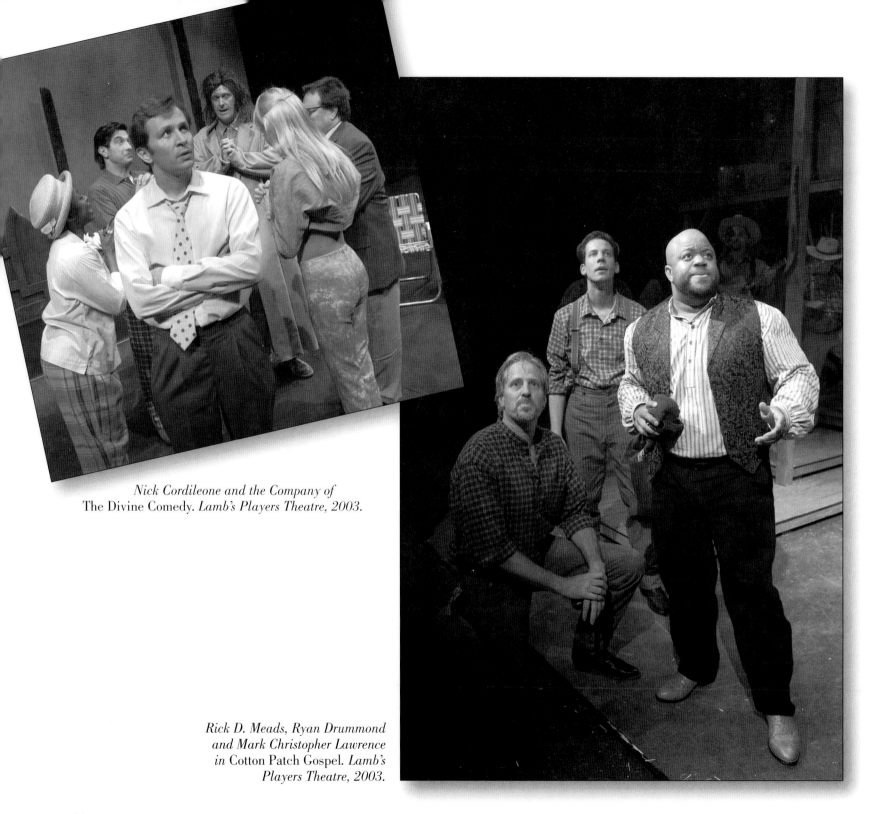

Nick Cordileone and the Company of
The Divine Comedy. *Lamb's Players Theatre, 2003.*

Rick D. Meads, Ryan Drummond
and Mark Christopher Lawrence
in Cotton Patch Gospel. *Lamb's*
Players Theatre, 2003.

D.W. Jacobs and Darla Cash in Three Hotels.
San Diego Repertory Theatre, 1994.

Darla and I worked with Todd Salovey on this brightly intelligent play about deeply tragic events. In this play, the genteel and wealthy members of the global corporate culture float atop vast and filthy swamps of poverty and crime. They learn how easy it is for their nearest and dearest to slip down, through and away. A deeply prophetic play, I'm afraid.

— *D.W. Jacobs, Actor, Playwright, Director*

The time was the mid '80s. The play was *Bent* by Martin Sherman. The director was Ginny-Lynn Safford (later to become Glyn Bedington). The theatre was the Bowery. And the production blew my mind.

It was intense, riveting, thought-provoking. I couldn't get it out of my mind. I still can't. It was about a piece of history I had never known -- the brutal treatment of homosexuals in the Holocaust concentration camps. It stuck with me, gnawed at me. I felt compelled to tell everyone in San Diego that they had to see this production. On a whim, on the crazy, what-the-hell advice of a friend, I took my review to KPBS, my passion for the piece spilling all over the page and oozing out of my pores. They liked the energy. I guess they still do. I've been on their airwaves for two decades.

After years of reviewing San Diego productions, I wanted to give something back to the theatre community. So in 1997, I created the Patté Awards for Theatre Excellence, to offer some tangible appreciation of the creative energy, the exhaustive hours, the tireless commitment and endless entertainment provided by local theatremakers — writers, actors, directors and designers — the talented people who bring their art, their craft and their heart to San Diego stages.

It was passion that drew me to the theatre as a child and passion that keeps me going more than 150 times a year now — to small theatres and large, to see classics, new works and wild experiments. Theatre has the power to change lives. San Diego theatre changed mine.

— *Pat Launer, theatre critic, KPBS*

Above and below right: *Company of* Bent. *The Bowery Theatre, 1986.*

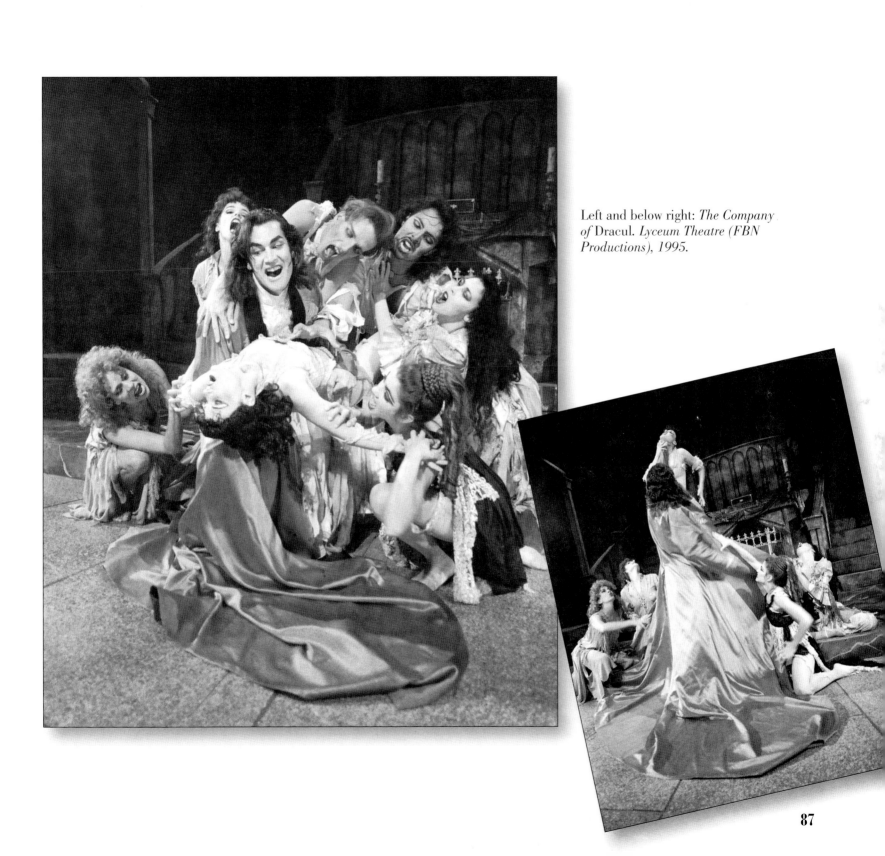

Left and below right: *The Company of* Dracul. *Lyceum Theatre (FBN Productions), 1995.*

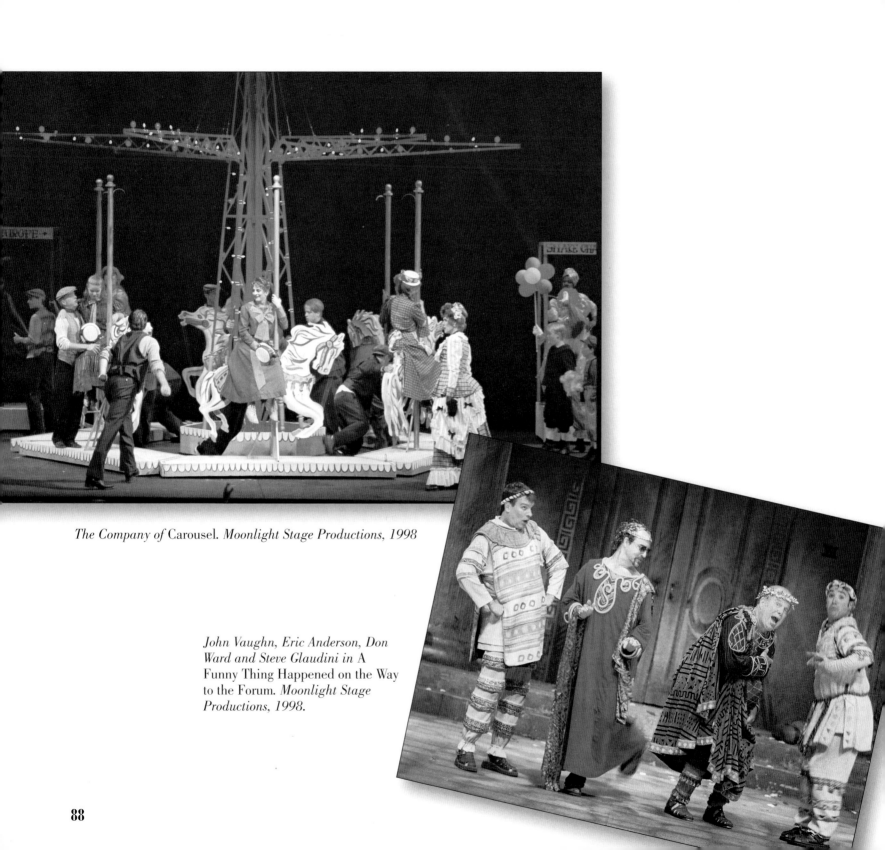

The Company of Carousel. *Moonlight Stage Productions, 1998*

John Vaughn, Eric Anderson, Don Ward and Steve Glaudini in A Funny Thing Happened on the Way to the Forum. *Moonlight Stage Productions, 1998.*

Above:
*J. Sherwood
Montgomery and
Douglin Murray Schmidt in*
The Pirates of Penzance.
Lyric Opera San Diego, 2003.

Left: *J. Sherwood Montgomery in*
The Pirates of Penzance.
Lyric Opera San Diego, 2003.

89

Above: *Mike Genovese in* Death of a Salesman. *San Diego Repertory Theatre, 1998.*
Right: *Mike Genovese and Barbara Tarbuck in* Death of a Salesman. *San Diego Repertory Theatre, 1998.*
Below: *Mike Genovese, Michael Hummel, Barbara Tarbuck and Douglas Roberts* Death of a Salesman. *San Diego Repertory Theatre, 1998.*

Sabrina LaBeauf and Matte Osian in A Streetcar Named Desire. *San Diego Repertory Theatre, 1996.*

Matte Osian and Sabrina LaBeauf in A Streetcar Named Desire. *San Diego Repertory Theatre, 1996.*

91

The moment I stood in front of St. Cecilia's Playhouse, the home of Sledgehammer Theatre, I knew I wasn't just going to see a play, but an event. There was a sense of anticipation as I waited with the other audience members in front of the former funeral chapel. I wasn't the only one who was nervous, scared, and exhilarated by what lay behind the double doors. We all looked at each other, knowing that we would be sharing a one-of-a-kind experience. We took our seats and the show began. By the time the performance had ended, I was exhausted and awestruck. Sledgehammer forced me to actively watch the piece, to give part of myself to the process, just as the actors were giving themselves to the play and the audience. I realized this is where I wanted to be. This is where theatre happens.

The Company of Kid-Simple. *Sledgehammer Theatre, 2004.*

That was 1990. When I became the Artistic Director of Sledgehammer in 1999, I wanted everyone to feel the same way I did that first time I walked through the doors. I made it my mission to create theatrical events — to turn theatre on its head and brazenly push the art form to new heights. Many of the theatre venues in San Diego are beautiful; but none inspire like St. Cecilia's. She forces you to break out of conventional thinking and look at a theatrical spaces in new, innovative ways each time you approach a project. She takes no prisoners and demands only the finest. That is the beauty of the space and the beauty of theatre.

— *Kirsten Brant,*
Artistic Director,
Sledgehammer Theatre

Tim Dahlberg and Douglas Roberts in Lone Star and Laundry
and Bourbon. *The Bowery Theatre, 1986.*

93

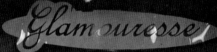

Above and left:
The Company of Pageant.
North Coast Repertory Theatre, 2002.

When *Six Women With Brain Death, or Expiring Minds Want To Know* opened in late October 1994, I said to Sam Woodhouse, "Let's run this show until my birthday!" Shows never ran for more than 9 or 10 weeks then, and my birthday falls in late August, so I knew I was being a bit cocky, but the show kept selling out. Women would stop those of us in the cast in grocery stores, saying they had seen the show 3,4, 5 times, and they were bringing their friends back again. The show was still going strong on my birthday and continued for almost 2 years. It was quite a phenomenon. We sang the National Anthem at a Chargers game and Mayor Maureen O'Connor designated a "Six Women with Brain Death Day." I lost count of the number of performances I did, but it was somewhere around 560. Other shows have since broken our long-running record, but I think we set the stage (if you will).

— *Linda Libby, Actor*

Left and Above: *The Company of* Six Women with Brain Death, or Expiring Minds Want to Know. *San Diego Repertory Theatre, 1996.*

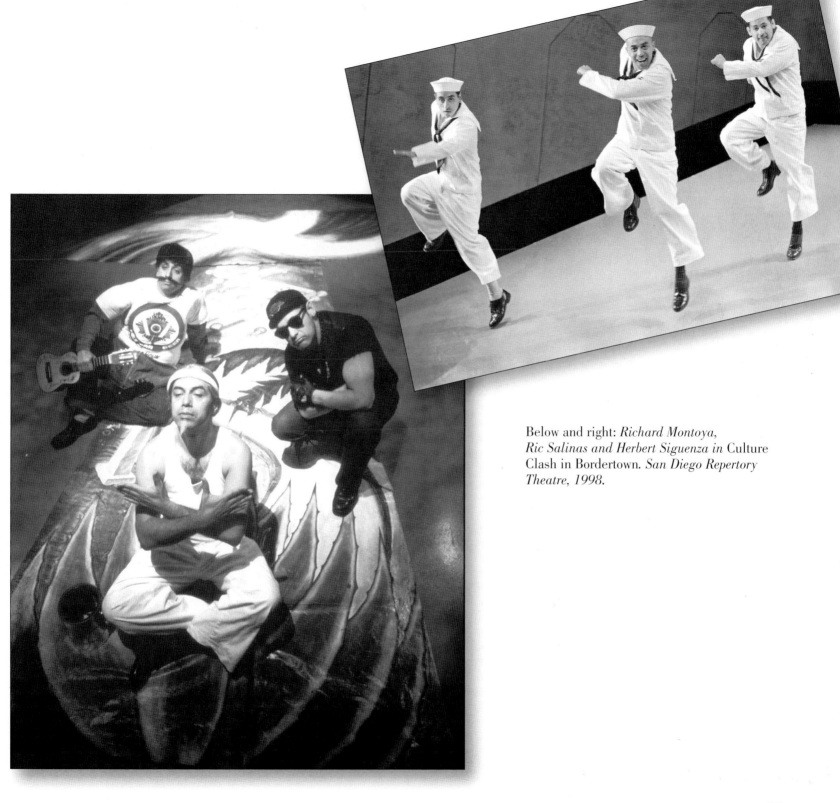

Below and right: *Richard Montoya,
Ric Salinas and Herbert Siguenza in* Culture
Clash in Bordertown. *San Diego Repertory
Theatre, 1998.*

Memoir was such a great opportunity—Katherine McGrath and I, two Globe Associate Artists who've been working together for thirty-some years, getting a chance to reunite (we'd done *Dear Liar* years before). My first year at the Globe was 1961 — and Kathy came a few years later, so we'd done dozens of plays together. It's just wonderful to work with someone who knows you so well, because you're able to connect so easily and to trust, and that enables you to take risks. Joseph Hardy, another Globe Associate Artist, directed the show, and the three of us worked together so happily, with a lot of love and trust.

The play is about Sarah Bernhardt's waning years—Kathy played Sarah, and I played her private secretary, Pitou, who was a real person…*Memoir* wasn't based on letters like *Dear Liar;* it was a more dramatic, more personal thing—full of pathos and humor. We loved doing it—so it was a happy reunion. And very successful, because people love to see us together…You work together enough, and you get to know each other's timing and depth, so you can get things out of your own performance you couldn't get otherwise. You don't have that sense of meeting a new person and not knowing what they are going to do… Katherine and I have a great onstage love for each other—and that comes across.
— *Jonathan McMurtry, Actor*

Katherine McGrath and Jonathan McMurtry in Memoir. *Old Globe Theatre, 2003.*

Linda Williams Janke, Lois Markle and Kathy Ireland in Three Tall Women. *San Diego Repertory Theatre, 1998.*

Ria Carey and Jill Lewis in
The Boyfriend. *Lyric Opera San Diego,*
2001.

The Company of
The Boyfriend.
Lyric Opera San
Diego, 2001.

The Company of Bessie's Blues.
San Diego Repertory Theatre, 1993.

The Company of Smokey Joe's Café. Moonlight Stage Productions, 2003.

Stan Chandler and Victoria Strong in Kiss Me, Kate. *Moonlight Stage Productions, 2004.*

102

The Company of Quilters. *San Diego Repertory Theatre, 1986.*

The Company of Slam. *San Diego Repertory Theatre, 2000.*

When I moved to San Diego, history was in the making but it seemed to be taking its sweet time. San Diego was seeking expression; that was clear. From the depths of the Gaslamp Quarter to the pit of National City, from the heart of Balboa Park to the developing Lawrence Welk Village, entertainment was being born. In the midst of this burgeoning artistic force, in the dingy corner of the Gaslamp district…was the Hahn Cosmopolitan Theatre, home to the Gaslamp Quarter Theatre Company. Under the Artistic Direction of Kit Goldman was a fantastic theatre that produced Mamet, Simon, Coward, and the first racially-mixed *Frankie and Johnny in the Claire de Lune.* I dressed every actor on that stage from 1989 till the mid 90's, thanks to the wonderful mentorship of Diane Holly.

In the last 20 years, I've had the honor of costuming at least 150 productions in San Diego. What has evolved is a collaboration of technicians from various theatre companies, including myself, teaming together at new venues like the small but mighty 6th@Penn Theatre and Sean Murray's emerging Cygnet Theatre, to create and produce wonderful new, and sometimes forgotten classic, plays…San Diego's arts community is experiencing the camaraderie in the spirit of art that has grown in this city.

It is the amity that I love and remember fondly as I look back on a town that has emerged from a struggling artistic community to being donned "Off Broadway West."
— *Jeanne Reith, Costume Designer*

Farhang Pernoon and Karl Backus in Gross Indecency: The Three Trials of Oscar Wilde. *Diversionary Theatre, 2003.*

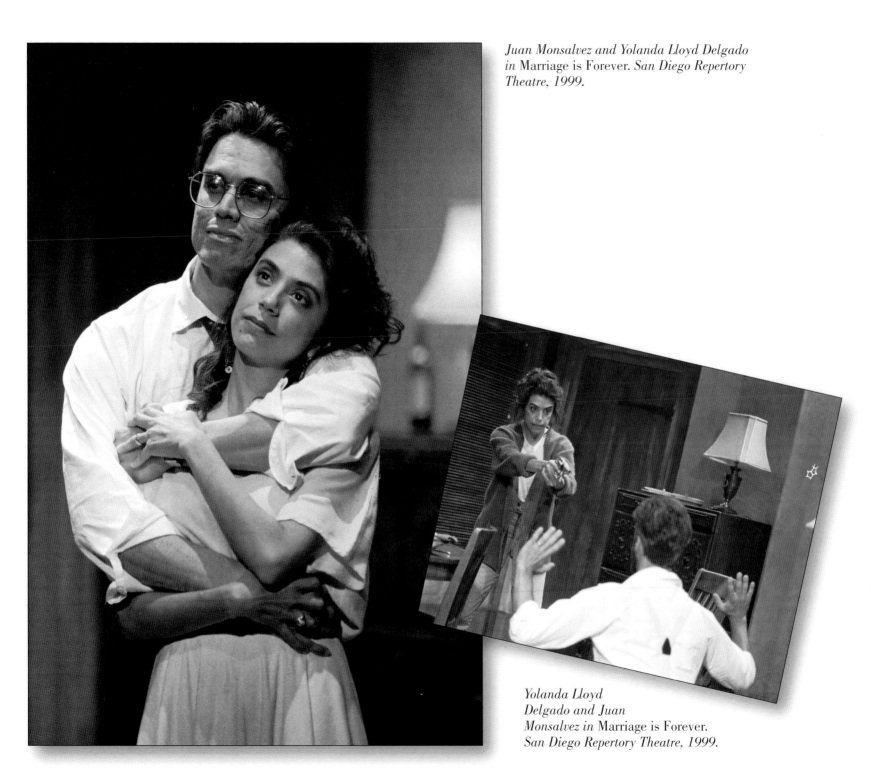

Juan Monsalvez and Yolanda Lloyd Delgado in Marriage is Forever. *San Diego Repertory Theatre, 1999.*

Yolanda Lloyd Delgado and Juan Monsalvez in Marriage is Forever. *San Diego Repertory Theatre, 1999.*

Robert Smyth, Paul Eggington and Tom Stephenson in Art. *Lamb's Players Theatre in 2004*

I believe in the magic of theatre — of great stories that explore the principles that shape our existence: love, laughter, pain, joy, greed; the comedy of being human; the dark and the light; despair and hope. For me, that magic is realized in the almost-impossible way that the theatre forces you to work together toward a goal — forces community between the artists and then spreads out to the final character in the performance: the audience.

Theatre is here and gone — no matter how fabulous a show is, it must end. The performance arts, to me, operate like the here-and-gone reality of our lives. I always feel a little sad when a great show closes. The 'lifetime' of that work is past and you look ahead to the birth of the new...

I'm also one who is enormously moved and fed by visual art — that art that lives on physically after the artist is gone — so I am grateful that Ken Jacques has spent so much of his talent chronicling the performance art of this great city.

— *Debbie Smyth, actor*

Robert Smyth and Keith Jefferson in The Boys Next Door. *Lamb's Players Theatre, 2003.*

Robert Smyth and Deborah Gilmour Smyth in The Boys Next Door. *Lamb's Players Theatre, 2003.*

Above: *The Company of* El Paso Blue. *San Diego Repertory Theatre, 1994.*

Below: *Pace Ebbeson, Delia MacDougall and Vic Trevino in* El Paso Blue. *San Diego Repertory Theatre, 1994.*

Lawrence Hecht and Jennifer Parsons in How I Learned to Drive. *San Diego Repertory Theatre, 1998.*

Left: *Vic Trevino in* El Paso Blue. *San Diego Repertory Theatre, 1994.*

The great boom in San Diego theatre began in the 1980s and it hasn't stopped since.

As a teen-ager, I remember attending low-budget performances of San Diego Repertory Theatre's *A Christmas Carol*, never realizing that the company's annual productions of the Dickens classic (now rich with original music, special effects, Equity casts and elaborate costumes) would still be attracting thousands of ticket-buyers some 28 years later.

And as a college student, I remember buying tickets to the then-little-known La Jolla Playhouse, which rock singer-turned-artistic director Des McAnuff had bravely revived in 1983. The first show I saw there was McAnuff's gorgeous staging of *As You Like It* starring Amanda Plummer and the biggest man-made tree I'd ever seen crammed inside a theatre. I knew it would be hard to equal that staging or Plummer's transcendent performance anytime or anywhere.

— *Pam Kragen, Critic*

Angie Phillips and David Hunt in Thérèse Raquin. *La Jolla Playhouse, 1996.*

Above: *Ron Campbell in*
R. Buckminster Fuller:
The History (and Mystery)
of the Universe. *San Diego
Repertory Theatre, 2000.*

Left: *Ollie Nash in* The
Strange Case of Dr. Jekyll
and Mr. Hyde. *San Diego
Repertory Theatre, 1987.*

The Company of Dark as Night. *Sledgehammer Theatre, 1991.*

My love of and life in the theatre in San Diego began almost the same time my family arrived in the United States from Mexico City. It was November, 1951, and we came to live in Chula Vista, California. My mother, a well known *declamadora*, that is, an actress who recites poetry and monologues, was instrumental in teaching and encouraging me in music and theatre, and at the age of seven my father enrolled me in the first private acting school in San Diego, called the Actors' Quarters, directed by Thor Svenson.

That is when I met my mentor and guide at the Old Globe Theatre, Craig Noel. I have been involved with the Globe for over forty-five years, as a greeter, assistant director, director, artistic advisor for Teatro Meta, and actor. As I continued my education at San Diego State, I was fortunate enough to be in a generation of actors and directors who became very famous in theatre, television, film and musical theatre. Among them were Fred Dwyer, Julie Kavner, Carl Weathers, Bob Hays, and Hal Clement.

I have been extremely lucky to work in the visual and performing arts for all my life, and have been blessed by people who have seen, participated in, and been part of this creative process for over fifty-two years.

— *Bill Virchis,*
Actor and Director

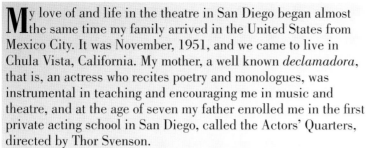

Above and Left: *Jorge Galvan in* Zoot Suit. *San Diego Repertory Theatre, 1997.*

There are no coincidences in life...I was in the waiting room at the V.A. Hospital in La Jolla reading in the military newspaper that the Coronado Playhouse was doing a production of *One Flew over the Cuckoo's Nest* and they were encouraging African American actors to audition. It was 1981, I was 31 and a closeted actor. I had dabbled in acting in college, keeping it a great secret from my football teammates. Although wanting very badly to investigate this invitation to "African American actors," I was afraid. I had never ventured to Coronado and, in my mind, attending the theatre there was something for white folks and the occasional Oreo person of color—I considered going, but my mistrust of the world stopped me in my tracks and I put it out of mind. A few days later, a co-worker told me that he knew the manager of the Playhouse and he could put in a good word for me, to be the volunteer bartender. That coincidence gave me the nerve I needed to venture to Coronado to volunteer as a bartender and at least see what it was like to be around theatre folks. Upon entering the theatre that day, artistic director Tom McCrory asked me to audition because "we don't get a lot of black actors coming over to Coronado to audition." I did, and I won the part of Turkle. This began a journey that would be the most exciting time of my life and give me the opportunity to find out who I am and why I'm here on this earth.

Doren Elias and David S. Humphrey in South Pacific. *Lamb's Players Theatre, 2004.*

Doren Elias, Jim Mooney, Antonio "TJ" Johnson and Linda Libby in South Pacific. *Lamb's Players Theatre, 2004.*

114

Over the years, I have crossed paths with hundreds of entertainers, performed in front of thousands and felt the love of every one of them. I've watched and experienced the growth of San Diego theatre. I've seen the foundations of diversity grow through the passion, care, and imagination of the pioneers building the San Diego theatre community. I've watched with excitement and frustration as the community of theatre has struggled and struggled to finally become a national influence. I've become a part of the family of actors, directors, supporters, founders, and critics. All of it is captured in Ken's images over the years. All of it has served to build bridges to an exciting future for the next generation of performers and theatre-goers of all orientations. The bridges to diversity have been crossed, the gateway for all actors has been opened. In the 80's, the word was that if you were an actor of color, to have a career you would need to leave San Diego. I am so glad I stayed.

— *T.J. Johnson, Actor*

Stephen Godwin and Erica Beth Phillips in South Pacific. *Lamb's Players Theatre, 2004.*

The Company of Sylvia. Old Globe Theatre, 1995.

Bill Anton and Kellie Waymire in Sylvia. *Old Globe Theatre, 1996.*

116

The Company of Peter Pan. *Moonlight Stage Productions, 1999.*

The Company
of Peter Pan.
Moonlight Stage
Productions,
1999.

Above and right: *The Company of* Avenue X.
San Diego Repertory Theatre, 1998.

Monica Quintanilla and Peggy Blow in Crowns.
San Diego Repertory Theatre, 2004.

Karole Foreman, Lisa H. Payton and
Charyn Cannon in Crowns. *San Diego*
Repertory Theatre, 2004.

Tom Zohar, Christopher Williams and Robert Grossman in The Chosen. *North Coast Repertory Theatre, 2004.*

Christopher Williams, Tom Zohar and Ralph Elias in The Chosen. *North Coast Repertory Theatre, 2004.*

The Company of Installation. *6th Avenue Playhouse 1991.*

For over twenty-five years, I have had the remarkable opportunity to learn about theatre by building a theatre company. Lamb's Players incorporated in 1971 as a touring troupe and quickly built a strong reputation for funny, fast-paced, physical street theatre — performing modern morality plays on college campuses nationwide. I joined the organization in 1976, an idealistic twenty-something with a crazy vision to start a resident repertory company — a group committed to exploring work together over an extended period. We opened our first resident theatre in National City in 1978 and it has been an adventurous ride ever since.

I marvel at the theatre community built here over the last twenty-five years and at the legacies built by Craig, Jack, Des, Doug and Sam. San Diego now boasts four major professional companies, and a diverse group of semi-professional houses.

When a piece of theatre works, there is no other experience quite like it.

— *Robert Smyth,*
Artistic Director,
Lamb's Players Theatre

Above: *Matt Scott, Rick D. Meads, Jennifer Austin and David Cochran Heath in* Dial M for Murder. *Lamb's Players Theatre, 2004.*
Right: *Matt Scott, Jennifer Austin and David Cochran Heath in* Dial M for Murder. *Lamb's Players Theatre, 2004.*

We do not spring from the womb full-blown and spouting iambic pentameter in a plea for pap. *Waaa* will do.

Admittedly, most things in life are learned slowly. Take theatrical criticism.

"I'm going out of town for a few weeks and there are some plays opening at the Old Globe that I'd like you to cover," said *Daily Californian* editor Dan Taylor in 1981. "The first is *King Lear* and it opens tonight."

I'd seen David Ogden Stiers on TV, read Julius Caesar in high school, and seen *The Taming of the Shrew* a few years before. Deep within, I knew that these did not competency make, so I did what any wise and foolish person would do: I went to the downtown library to look up *Lear*. That night I sat in the dark trying to keep the characters straight. Lear had three daughters. Who the heck were they married to and who did what to whom? And Edgar and Edmund: which was bad, which good?

Despite my ill preparedness and my terror of having to write about *Lear*, the magic overtook me. Blessedly my first *Lear* review is not where I can lay hands on't. Otherwise, I'd die of mortification.

I've encountered *Lear* many times throughout the years, memorably Hal Holbrook's at the Globe in 1993, the late Richard Kneeland's at Chicago Shakespeare later the same year, and, most affectingly, in three summers ago at the San Francisco Shakespeare Festival, where Lear, Gloucester, and the Fool were played by men in their 70s.

For good or ill, even though I'm still learning, Lear owns me now.

— *Charlene Baldridge, Theatre Critic*

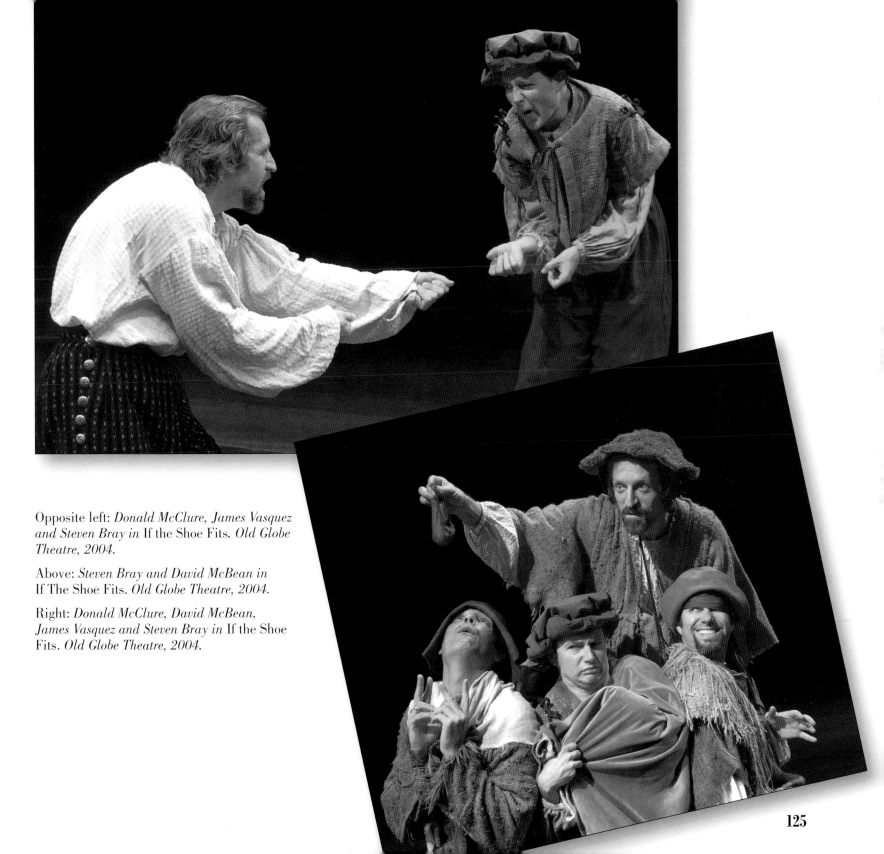

Opposite left: *Donald McClure, James Vasquez and Steven Bray in* If the Shoe Fits. *Old Globe Theatre, 2004.*

Above: *Steven Bray and David McBean in* If The Shoe Fits. *Old Globe Theatre, 2004.*

Right: *Donald McClure, David McBean, James Vasquez and Steven Bray in* If the Shoe Fits. *Old Globe Theatre, 2004.*

1989

Various Companies of A Christmas Carol.
San Diego Repertory Theatre.

1993

1997

1984

126

A Christmas Carol...

We have been doing this show for almost 30 years. The many different productions were like executing variations on a theme. Over decades, vast multitudes have brought their talents to this show. The first Tiny Tim is in his late thirties by now.

I came from a family with five children. All my aunts and uncles had at least five children. Holidays roared like a freight train in our family. Much of my own holiday experiences found their way into this script. It was my father who kept bugging me to do an adaptation of Dickens' classic tale. We first opened it in 1976 at San Diego City College. That year, Lyman Saville, Dave Diller, Lynne Mayfield, and President Alan Repashy opened the doors of the San Diego City College theatre. We did most of the Rep's first season there. I will always be grateful for their hospitality and generosity. They offered to give us the theatre for the summer, but we had to be incorporated as a non–profit.

In two months, Sam and I incorporated the theatre, applied for the tax exemptions, chose three plays, hired directors and designers, cast the plays, marketed them, began rehearsals and opened the first production of the 1976 Summer Comedy Festival. At that time, the Rep was in the process of growing sideways out from Indian Magique, the legendary San Diego street theatre

1987

1996

1972

1988

group. Willa Mann first plugged in at that time to become Stage Manager, Lighting Designer, and rapidly assumed the role of Production Manager. We were younger then. It seemed like we could do anything in two months. Later that same year, two months was the time it took to do the first *Christmas Carol*, from conception to opening night. It took just two months from the lease-signing with Virginia Robertson, to renovate and convert the St. Cecilia's Funeral Chapel into a Playhouse and hit the opening night of the 2ⁿᵈ San Diego Summer Comedy Festival. The Piparoos were born on that same fateful June night.

But it was the night before we opened our world premiere of *A Christmas Carol*, when Willa, Sam and I found ourselves in the emergency room of University Hospital. At the end of our final dress rehearsal, the huge plywood show sign dropped down onto the stage, and into the middle of the gathered cast and crew, like a piece of giant toast into a human toaster. The sign grazed Sam's hand, splitting his clipboard in two, and slid down the side of Sheldon Boyce's shoulder. No other injuries. A bit of a miracle. After leaving the hospital, we stayed up all night in a diner rewriting light cues. I played the Narrator to Bernard Baldan's Scrooge. Welton Jones called him a great bear of a Scrooge. And that was true. Being on stage with Bernard was like coming home.

— *D.W. Jacobs,*
Actor, Playwright, Director

2003

2003

2003

128

Ron Taylor in It Ain't Nothin' But the Blues.
San Diego Repertory Theatre, 2000.

The Company of It Ain't Nothin' But the Blues.
San Diego Repertory Theatre, 2000.

129

Right: Jessa Watson, Annie Hinton and James Saba in The Importance of Being Earnest. *North Coast Repertory Theatre, 2002.*
Below: Sean Murray in Travesties. *North Coast Repertory Theatre, 2002.*

Left: James Saba, Jeffrey Jones, Sean Murray, and Jim Chovick in Travesties. *North Coast Repertory Theatre, 2002.*

130

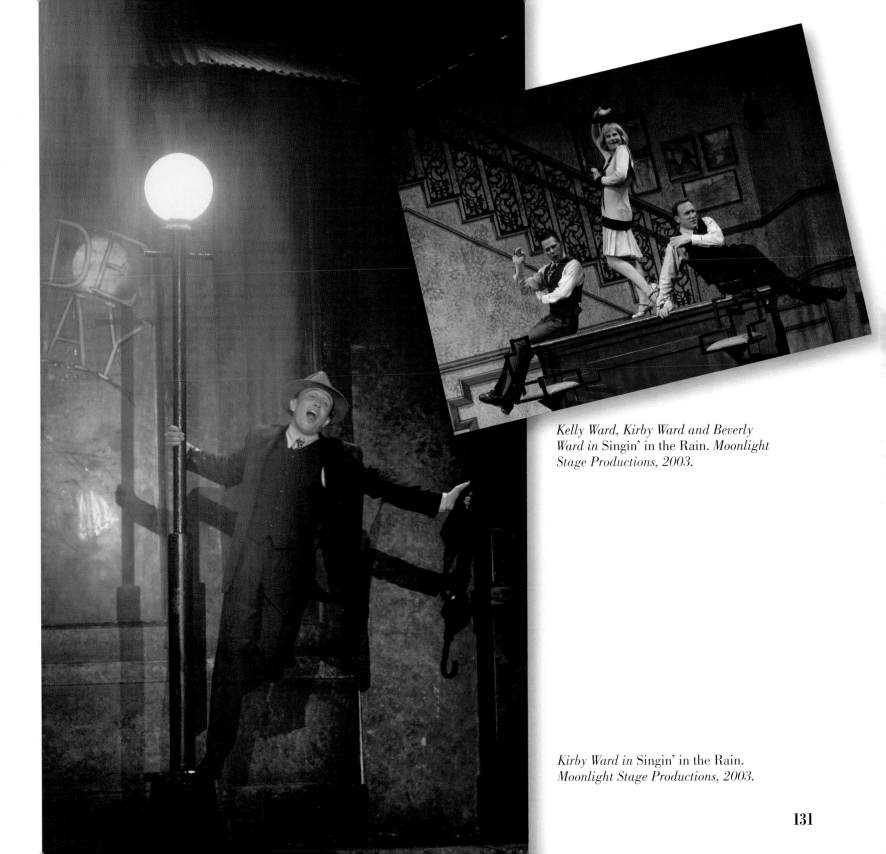

Kelly Ward, Kirby Ward and Beverly Ward in Singin' in the Rain. *Moonlight Stage Productions, 2003.*

Kirby Ward in Singin' in the Rain. *Moonlight Stage Productions, 2003.*

Lakin Valdez and Alma Martinez in Mummified Deer. *San Diego Repertory Theatre, 2001.*

The Company of The Great Divorce. Lamb's Players Theatre, 2003.

Tom Stephenson in Dr. Faustus. Lamb's Players Theatre, 2003.

133

Robin Gammell and Robert Foxworth in Julius Caesar. *Old Globe Theatre, 2003.*

Robert Foxworth and Robin Gammell in Julius Caesar. *Old Globe Theatre, 2003.*

134

Annie Berthiaume, Edward Staudenmayer and T. Eric Hart in The Scarlet Pimpernel. *Starlight Musical Theatre, 2003.*

*Linda Libby and Seema Sueko
in* Remains. *Mo'olelo Performing Arts
Company, 2004.*

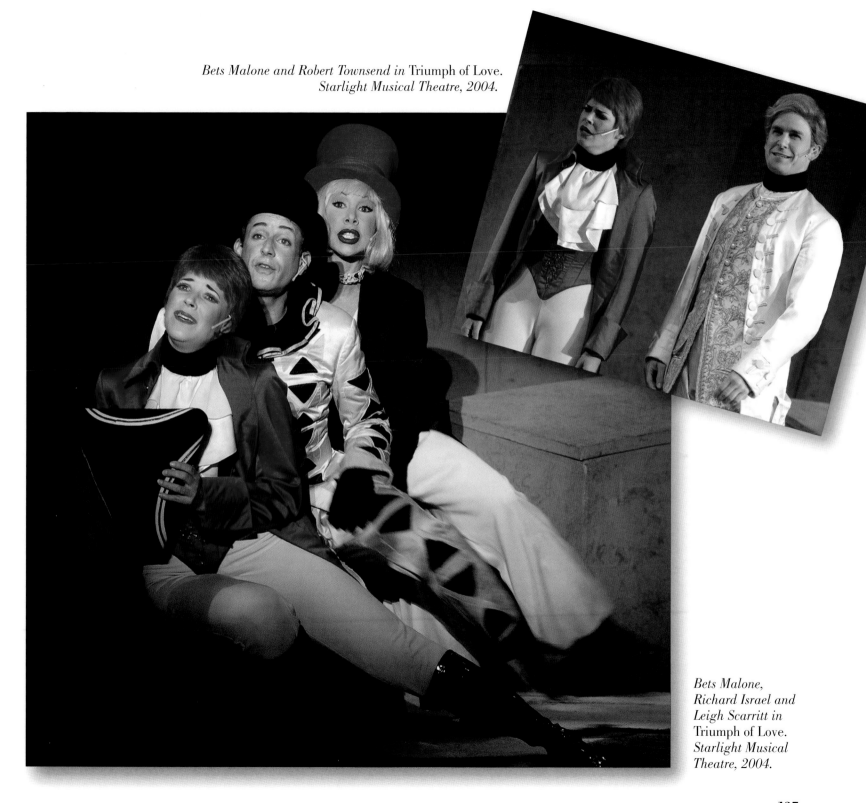

Bets Malone and Robert Townsend in Triumph of Love. *Starlight Musical Theatre, 2004.*

Bets Malone, Richard Israel and Leigh Scarritt in Triumph of Love. *Starlight Musical Theatre, 2004.*

137

The Company of Three Mo' Divas. *San Diego Repertory Theatre, 2004.*

The Company of Sky Girls. *The Old Globe Theatre, 2003.*

Kirsten Benton Chandler in Sweet Charity. *Moonlight Stage Productions, 2003.*

140

Kirsten Benton Chandler in Sweet Charity.
Moonlight Stage Productions, 2003.

The Company of Ain't Misbehavin'.
Moonlight Stage Productions, 2003.

The Company of Cabaret. *North Coast Repertory Theatre, 2002.*

Jeremiah Lorenz in Cabaret. *North Coast Repertory Theatre, 2002.*

Diep Huynh in M. Butterfly. *Diversionary Theatre, 2003.*

Priscilla Allen, Laura Bozanich and Jenni Prisk in The Killing of Sister George. *Diversionary Theatre, 2003.*

143

Above and below right: The Company of Macbeth. *Sledgehammer Theatre, 2004.*

Janet Hayatshahi and David Tierney in Macbeth. *Sledgehammer Theatre, 2004.*